ROUGH GUIDES **PHRASEBOOK**

JAPANESE

ROUGH
GUIDES

Contacting the Editors

Every effort has been made to provide accurate information in this publication, but changes are inevitable. The publisher cannot be responsible for any resulting loss, inconvenience or injury.
We would appreciate it if readers would call our attention to any errors or outdated information. We also welcome your suggestions; if you come across a relevant expression not in our phrase book, please contact us at: **hello@insightguides.com**

All Rights Reserved
© 2019 APA Publications (UK) Ltd.

Cover & Interior Design: Slawomir Krajewski
Head of Production: Rebeka Davies
Production Manager: Rebecca Hancock
Picture Researcher: Slawomir Krajewski
Cover Photo: all shutterstock

Interior Photos: all shutterstock

CONTENTS

INTRODUCTION

PRACTICALITIES

ON THE WAY

LEISURE TIME

SAFE TRAVEL

FOOD

PEOPLE

DICTIONARY

PRONUNCIATION

This section is designed to familiarize you with the sounds of Japanese using simplified phonetic transcription. The pronunciation of the Japanese sounds is explained below, together with their 'imitated' equivalents. This system is used throughout the phrase book. When you see a word spelled phonetically, simply read the pronunciation as if it were English, noting any special rules.

Japanese is a unique language. Apart from a similarity of script (the Japanese adopted Chinese ideograms) it bears no resemblance to Chinese or other Asian languages, except for Korean. Where Japanese comes from is still a matter of conjecture. Japan, its people, customs, and language were almost totally isolated until the late nineteenth century. Today there are many foreign 'loan' words that have been adopted into Japanese. From **pan** (from the Portuguese for bread) to **sportsman**, you will come across many foreign words, the majority of which are from English. At first hearing, you may not recognize these words because of the change in pronunciation and, conversely, you may not be understood when using a 'loan' word until you give it a Japanese pronunciation.

Japanese is composed less of vowels and consonants than of syllables, consisting of a consonant and a vowel. Consonants are always followed by vowels, except for **n**, which can occur alone. All syllables are pronounced with equal force: there is no stress except for emphasis.

CONSONANTS

Letter	Approximate Pronunciation	Symbol	Example	Pronunciation
b	approximately as in English	b	バス	*basu*
ch	approximately as in English	ch	お茶	*ocha*

Letter	Approximate Pronunciation	Symbol	Example	Pronunciation
d	approximately as in English	d	電車	*densha*
g	approximately as in English	d	外国	*gaikoku*
h	approximately as in English	h	箱根	*hakone*
j	approximately as in English	j	原宿	*harajuku*
k	approximately as in English	k	観光	*kankoo*
m	approximately as in English	m	鎌倉	*kamakura*
p	approximately as in English	p	乾杯	*kanpai*
s	approximately as in English	s	寿司	*sushi*
t	approximately as in English	t	成田	*narita*

Letter	Approximate Pronunciation	Symbol	Example	Pronunciation
f	with lips flattened and without putting lower teeth against lower lip, between an f and an h	f	お風呂	*ofuro*
n	1. before vowels like n in now	n	長い	*nagai*
	2. at the end of a word, said without letting your tongue touch the roof of your mouth	n	さん	*san*

r	with tip of tongue against the gum behind the upper front teeth, between an r and an 1	r	りんご	*ringo*
w [semi-vowel]	the lips are not rounded but left slack	w	分かる	*wakaru*

Letter	Approximate Pronunciation	Symbol	Example	Pronunciation
z	1.at the beginning of words, like ds in beds	z	ゼロ	*zero*
	2. In the middle of words like z in zoo	z	水	*mizu*

Double consonants should be pronounced 'long', i.e. hold the sound for a moment. The doubling of a consonant is important as it can change the meaning of a word.

kk	一個	*ikko*
pp	かっぱ	*kappa*
tt	ちょっと	*chotto*

VOWELS

Letter	Approximate Pronunciation	Symbol	Example	Pronunciation
A	like the a in father, Pronounced forward in the mouth	a	魚	*sakana*
e	like e in get	e	テレビ	*terebi*
i	like i in sit	i	イギリス	*igirisu*
o	like o in note	o	男	*otoko*
u	like u in put, but without rounding the lips	u	冬	*fuyu*

Long vowels (**aa**, **ee**, **ii**, **oo**, **uu**) are held for twice the amount of time. This is important in Japanese and can change the meaning of words, e.g. **oba(san)** means aunt while **obaa(san)** means grandmother.

Vowel clusters: when two vowels occur together (**ie, ai, ue, ao**) they should be pronounced separately with each vowel keeping its normal sound.

Consonant/double vowel clusters: (e.g. **kya, kyu, kyo**) these are two sounds said quickly so that they become one: **kya** is **ki** and **ya**.

Whispered vowels: sometimes **i** and **u** are devoiced, that is whispered or even omitted. This happens when **i** and **u** occur at the end of a word, or between voiceless consonants: **ch, f, h, k, p, s, sh, t**, and **ts**.

Japanese is composed of three different 'scripts' or ways of writing: **kanji** (Chinese characters or ideograms), **hiragana** (an alphabet in which each symbol represents a spoken syllable), and **katakana** (another alphabet).These three systems are used in combination to write modern Japanese. **Hiragana** is used to link **kanji** characters together. **Katakana** is used to write foreign 'loan' words, most of which are English in origin.

In addition to these three 'scripts' you will find **romaji**, the Romanized system used to write Japanese. In Japan important signs and names are often given in **romaji**, for example the names of subway stations.

Traditionally Japanese is written from the top to the bottom of the page starting in the upper right-hand corner. Today it is also commonly written horizontally and from left to right. The Japanese phrases you will see in this book incorporate a mixture of **kanji**, **hiragana** and **katakana**, and the pronunciation is in **romaji**. Japanese words and phrases are pronounced very evenly, and stress is used only to emphasize meaning. Pitch does vary however; normal sentences will begin on a high note and finish on a low note. As in English, questions normally rise in pitch at the end of the sentence.

HOW TO USE THE APP

Quickly access your recently viewed entries

Look up words and phrases on-the-go

Conveniently navigate the phrasebook categories

Change font size and background color

No SIM 17.55

ROUGH GUIDES

Spanish Phrasebook

Getting Started >

Exploring >

Activities >

Health & Safety >

Food & Drink >

Menu reader >

Going out

Phrasebook   Tools   Catalogue   Favourites   Info

Save the most useful everyday words and phrases to your Favorites

Use the Flash Cards Quiz to learn and memorize new words easily

Take all digital advantages of the app: listen to words and phrases pronounced by native speakers

To learn how to Activate the app, see the inside back cover of this phrasebook.

GRAMMAR

REGULAR VERBS

At first glance Japanese verbs are very straightforward, with only present and past tenses and no special form to indicate person or number. Future tense is gauged from the context.

However, verbs are subject to other changes to express variety of degrees of politeness and mood. The two basic verb forms are:

taberu	to eat	**nomu**	to drink
tabemasu	to eat	**nomimasu**	to drink
(polite form)		(polite form)	

This phrase book uses the polite form throughout.

tabemasu	(I, you, he, she, we, they) eat
tabemasen	(I, you, he, she, we, they) don't/doesn't eat
tabemashita	(I, you, he, she, we, they) ate
tabemasendeshita	(I, you, he, she, we, they) didn't eat

In addition to the above forms, verbs can indicate such functions as causative, command, conditional, passive, potential etc. by adding appropriate suffixes. For example:

tabesasemasu	I cause (someone) to eat
tabero!	Eat!
tabereba	if you eat...

PARTICLES

Japanese uses a number of particles to mark the use, or add to the meaning of the word they follow in a sentence.

ga	subject marker	**nodo ga itai desu**	literal meaning: The throat is sore.
wa	attention-directing marker	**watashi wa nodo ga itai desu**	literal meaning: As for me the throat is sore.

| o | object marker | **gohan o tabemasu** | literal meaning: I eat rice. |

IRREGULAR VERBS

Japanese has only two irregular verbs: **suru** (to do) and **kuru** (to come). Their polite forms are as follows:

shimasu	do	**kimasu**	come
shimasen	don't/ doesn't do	**kimasen**	don't/ doesn't come
shimashita	did	**kimashita**	came
shimasendeshita	didn't do	**kimasendeshita**	didn't come

NOUNS & ARTICLES

Japanese nouns have no articles, and no plurals. All nouns have one single form that does not change according to the noun's role in a sentence.

Personal pronouns are used sparingly in Japanese. Use the person's name + **san** instead of a pronoun, or omit the pronoun completely if it is clear who is being addressed or referred to. Personal pronouns are:

watashib	I	**anata*** (singular)	you
watashi tachi	we	**anatagata*** (plural)	you

* These pronouns are very familiar and appropriate only between husband and wife or boyfriend and girlfriend.

WORD ORDER

Japanese questions are formed by adding the particle **ka** (a verbal question mark) to the verb at the end of a sentence. Note that in Japanese the verb always comes last. The basic rule for word order within a sentence is: subject – object – verb

Watashi wa Smith desu.   I'm (Mr./Mrs.) Smith.

Honda-san* desu ka?   Are you (Mr./Mrs.) Honda?

*When addressing a Japanese person you should use the family name followed by san. (Do not use san when referring to yourself!)

IMPERATIVES

There are many ways to indicate an order, depending on how strong you would like it to be. Following is an example of imperative from mild to strong:

Go!   **Itte**   **Ikinasai**   **Ike**

COMPARATIVE & SUPERLATIVE

Unlike English, Japanese adjectives do not indicate comparative or superlative. Instead Japanese employs the following pattern:

Comparative: **A to B to dochira ga** adjective **desuka?**

Tookyoo to Oosaka to dochira ga ookii desu ka.

Which is bigger, Tokyo or Osaka?

Superlative: **A to B to C de A ga ichiban** adjective **desu.**

Tookyoo to Oosaka to Kyooto de Tookyoo ga ichiban ookii desu.

Among Tokyo, Osaka and Kyoto, Tokyo is the biggest.

POSSESSIVE PRONOUNS

To make possessive pronouns, use the grammar marker **no** following the person's name or the personal pronoun.
Honda-san no hon   Mr./Mrs. Honda's book
Watashi no hon   my book

ADJECTIVES

A Japanese adjective ends in **i** and modifies a noun that is placed immediately after it. For example, 'a big room' will be **ookii** heya. Japanese adjectives are very different from their English counter parts, and behave more like verbs. The past tense of most adjectives is formed by adding **-katta** to the basic stem:

takai	expensive	**yasui**	cheap
takakatta	(was) expensive	**yasukatta**	(was) cheap

There is another group of adjectives that takes **na** at the end of the word to modify a noun.
Example: **kiree-na hana** (pretty flower), **taisetsu-na mono** (an important thing), **shizuka-na tokoro** (a quiet place).

ADVERBS

An adverb describes a verb. Many Japanese adverbs end in **ku**, and are derived from adjectives by replacing the final **i** of an adjective with **ku**.
Example: **Hayaku hashirimashita.** He ran quickly.

PRACTICALITIES

THE BASICS

NUMBERS

NEED TO KNOW

0	零/ゼロ
	ree/zero
1	一
	ichi
2	二
	ni
3	三
	san
4	四
	shi/yon
5	五
	go
6	六
	roku
7	七
	shichi/nana
8	八
	hachi
9	九
	kyuu/ku
10	十
	juu
11	十一
	juuichi
12	十二
	juuni

13	十三
	juusan
14	十四
	juushi/juuyon
15	十五
	juugo
16	十六
	juuroku
17	十七
	juushichi/juunana
18	十八
	juuhachi
19	十九
	juukyuu/juuku
20	二十
	nijuu
21	二十一
	nijuuichi
22	二十二
	nijuuni
30	三十
	sanjuu
31	三十一
	sanjuuichi
40	四十
	yonjuu/shijuu
50	五十
	gojuu
60	六十
	rokujuu
70	七十
	nanajuu/shichijuu

80	八十	*hachijuu*
90	九十	*kyuujuu*
100	百	*hyaku*
101	百一	*hyakuichi*
200	二百	*nihyaku*
500	五百	*gohyaku*
1,000	千	*sen*
10,000	一万	*ichiman*
1,000,000	百万	*hyakuman*

ORDINAL NUMBERS

first	一番	*ichiban*
second	二番	*niban*
third	三番	*sanban*
fourth	四番	*yonban*
fifth	五番	*goban*

once	一回	
	ikkai	
twice	二回	
	nikai	
three times	三回	
	sankai	

In Japanese, there are two ways of counting to ten. There are general numbers (listed on page 20) used for talking about sums of money, telephone numbers, etc. There is also a system for combining a number with an object-specific counter. This system groups objects into types according to shape and size. There are specific ways of counting flat objects, animals, people, etc. Luckily the counter system only applies to numbers from 1–10. After 10 the general number is used. When you are not sure of the correct counter, you can always use the 'all-purpose' counters listed below.

ALL PURPOSE COUNTERS (NUMBERS 1–10)

These counters are strictly used to count 'unclassifiable' objects (objects where shape or size are difficult to determine). When you don't know the specific counter use:

1	**hitotsu**	2	**futatsu**
3	**mittsu**	4	**yottsu**
5	**itsutsu**	6	**muttsu**
7	**nanatsu**	8	**yattsu**
9	**kokonotsu**	10	**too**

OTHER COUNTERS

Flat objects (stamps, paper, etc.)

1	**ichimai**	6	**rokumai**
2	**nimai**	7	**nanamai/ shichimai**
3	**sanmai**	8	**hachimai**
4	**yonmai**	9	**kyuumai**
5	**gomai**	10	**juumai**

People

1	**hitori**	6	**rokunin**
2	**futari**	7	**nananin/ shichinin**
3	**sannin**	8	**hachinin**
4	**yonin**	9	**kyuunin**
5	**gonin**	10	**juunin**

Long, thin objects (pen, bottle, umbrella, etc.)

1	**ippon**	6	**roppon**
2	**nihon**	7	**nanahon**
3	**sanbon**	8	**happon**
4	**yonhon**	9	**kyuuhon**
5	**gohon**	10	**juppon**

For example, the counter for a bottle is **nihon**.

I'd like two bottles of beer.   **Biru o nihon kudasai.**

If you didn't know the counter, you could use the 'all-purpose' counter:

I'd like two bottles of beer.   **Biiru o futatsu kudasai.**

Note that the counter usually follows the word it qualifies.

TIME

NEED TO KNOW

What time is it?	何時ですか。
	nanji desu ka
It's noon [midday].	十二時(正午)です。
	juuniji (shoogo) desu
At midnight.	真夜中に
	mayonaka ni
From nine o'clock to 5 o'clock.	九時から五時まで
	kuji kara goji made
Twenty [after] past four	四時二十分
	yoji nijuppun
A quarter to nine	九時十五分前
	kuji juugorun mae
5:30 a.m./p.m.	午前/午後五時三十分
	gozen/gogo goji sanjuppun

In ordinary conversation, time is expressed as shown above. For airline and train timetables, however, the 24-hour clock is used.

Japan is nine hours ahead of GMT all year round. Japan does not change its clocks to reflect winter and summer time.

DAYS

NEED TO KNOW

Sunday	日曜日 *nichiyoobi*
Monday	月曜日 *getsuyoobi*
Tuesday	火曜日 *kayoobi*
Wednesday	水曜日 *suiyoobi*
Thursday	木曜日 *mokuyoobi*
Friday	金曜日 *kinyoobi*
Saturday	土曜日 *doyoobi*

Japan changed from lunar calendar to the Gregorian calendar in 1873. However, the lunar calendar is still used in farming, and in other activities in rural areas of Japan. Japanese calendars start with Sunday and end with Saturday.

DATES

yesterday	昨日 *kinoo*
today	今日 *kyoo*

tomorrow	明日
	ashita
day	日
	nichi/hi
week	週
	shuu
month	月
	tsuki
year	年
	toshi

Dates in Japan are written in Year-Month-Day format. January 1st, 2010 would be **2010 年1月1日 nisen juu nen ichi gatsu tsuitachi**, or 2010, January, first.

MONTHS

January	一月
	ichigatsu
February	二月
	nigatsu
March	三月
	sangatsu
April	四月
	shigatsu
May	五月
	gogatsu
June	六月
	rokugatsu
July	七月
	shichigatsu

August	八月
	hachigatsu
September	九月
	kugatsu
October	十月
	juugatsu
November	十一月
	juuichigatsu
December	十二月
	juunigatsu

SEASONS

the spring	春
	haru
the summer	夏
	natsu
the fall [autumn]	秋
	aki
the winter	冬
	fuyu

HOLIDAYS

Public holidays
January 1 **ganjitsu/gantan** New Year's Day
Second Monday in January **seejin no hi** Adult's Day
February 11 **kenkoku kinen no hi** National Foundation Day
March 21* **shunbun no hi** Vernal Equinox Day
April 29 **midori no hi** Greenery Day
May 3 **kenpoo kinen bi** Constitution Day
May 5 **kodomo no hi** Children's Day
September 15 **keeroo no hi** Respect for the Aged Day
September 23* **shuubun no hi** Autumnal Equinox Day
October 10 **taiiku no hi** Health-Sports Day
November 3 **bunka no hi** Culture Day
November 23 **kinroo kansha no hi** Labor Thanksgiving Day
December 23 **tennoo tanjoobi** Emperor's Birthday
* These dates are lunar and change year by year.

The most important holiday in Japan is New Year's day.
All the stores are closed on the January first, and some will
close on the second and third as well. Adult's Day (second
Monday in January) is designated to celebrate those who
are and will be 20 during the year. The week from Greenery
Day (April 29) to Children's Day (May 5) is called the Golden
Week. Many people take advantage of the four holidays
falling during this week (Greenery Day, May Day, Constitution
Day, and Children's Day) to travel, thus creating traffic jams
everywhere. Bon Festival, from August 13 to 16, is a time
when many people go to their ancestral home: the souls
of the deceased ancestors are considered to come home
during this time.

ARRIVAL & DEPARTURE

NEED TO KNOW

I'm here on vacation [holiday]/business.	観光/仕事で来ました。 *kankoo/shigoto de kimashita*
I'm going to…	…へ行きます。 *…e ikimasu*
I'm staying at the… Hotel.	…ホテルに泊まっています。 *…hoteru ni tomatte imasu*

BORDER CONTROL

YOU MAY HEAR…

チケット/パスポートをお見せください。 *chiketto/pasupooto o omise kudasai*	Your ticket/ passport, please.
今回の旅行の目的は何ですか。 *konkai no ryokoo no mokuteki wa nan desu ka*	What's the purpose of your visit?
どこにお泊まりですか。 *doko ni otomari desu ka*	Where are you staying?
後、どのくらいいらっしゃいますか。 *ato donokurai irasshaimasu ka*	How long are you staying?
どなたとご一緒ですか。 *donata to goissho desu ka*	Who are you with?

I'm just passing through.	立ち寄るだけです。 *tachiyoru dake desu*

I would like to declare…	…を申告します。 *…o shinkoku shimasu*
I have nothing to declare.	申告するものはありません。 *shinkoku suru mono wa arimasen*

YOU MAY HEAR…

申告するものはありますか。
shinkoku suru mono wa arimasu ka

Do you have anything to declare?

関税がかかります。
kanzee ga kakarimasu

You must pay duty on this.

このバッグを開けてください。
kono baggu o akete kudasai

Please open this bag.

YOU MAY SEE…

税関検査 *zeekan kensa*	customs
免税品 *menzeehin*	duty-free goods
課税 *kazee*	goods to declare
免税 *menzee*	nothing to declare
入国手続き *nyuukoku tetsuzuki*	passport control
警察 *keesatsu*	police

MONEY

NEED TO KNOW

Where's...?	...はどこですか。
	...wa doko desu ka
the ATM	キャッシュコーナー
	kyasshu koonaa
the bank	銀行
	ginkoo
the currency exchange office	両替所
	ryoogaejo
What time does the bank open/close?	銀行は何時から/までですか。
	ginkoo wa nanji kara/made desu ka
I'd like to change dollars/pounds to yen	ル/ポンドを円に替えたいんですが。
	doru/pondo o en ni kaetain desu ga
I want to cash some traveler's checks [cheques].	トラベラーズチェックを換金したいんですが。
	toraberaazu chekku o kankin shitain desu ga

YOU MAY SEE...

カードを入れる	insert card
キャンセルする	cancel
消去する	clear
入力する	enter
暗証番号	PIN
引き出す	withdraw funds
当座預金口座から	from checking [current] account
普通預金口座から	from savings account
レシート/領収書	receipt

AT THE BANK

Can I exchange foreign currency here?	外国通貨の両替はできますか。 *gaikoku tsuuka no ryoogae wa dekimasu ka*
What's the exchange rate?	為替レートはいくらですか。 *kawase reeto wa ikura desu ka*
How much is the fee?	手数料はいくらですか。 *tesuuryoo wa ikura desu ka*
I've lost my traveler's checks [cheques].	トラベラーズチェックをなくしました。 *toraberaazu chekku o nakushimashita*
My card was lost.	カードをなくしました。 *kaado o nakushimashita*
My credit cards have been stolen.	クレジットカードを盗まれました。 *kurejitto kaado o nusumaremashita*
My card doesn't work.	カードが使えません。 *kaado ga tsukaemasen*

YOU MAY SEE...

The monetary system is the yen (円), abbreviated to ¥.
Coins: ¥1, ¥5, ¥10, ¥50, ¥100, and ¥500
Notes: ¥1,000, ¥2,000, ¥5,000, and ¥10,000

Banks are open from 9:00 a.m. to 5:00 p.m. Monday
through Friday. Some banks are open on Saturdays and
all banks are closed on Sundays, except the bank at Tokyo
Airport, which is open 24 hours a day.
Most banks have a foreign currency section. You will need to
show your passport to change foreign currency or traveler's
checks. You will usually be invited to sit down while the
transaction is conducted, which may take as long as 15
minutes. Your name will be called when your money is ready.
You will not be able to use foreign credit cards to get cash
from most ATMs, except those run by Citibank and the Japan
Post Bank postal service. Every post office in Japan has an
ATM where you can obtain cash using international credit
cards or cash cards from your bank. In rural areas, note that
banks may not have currency exchange facilities at all so the
safest solution is to have cash with you at all times.

CONVERSATION

NEED TO KNOW

Hello.	こんにちは 。
	konnichiwa
How are you?	お元気ですか。
	ogenki desu ka
Fine, thanks.	はい、おかげさまで。
	hai okage sama de
Excuse me! (to get attention)	失礼します。
	shitsuree shimasu
Do you speak English?	英語ができますか。
	eego ga dekimasu ka
What's your name?	お名前は。
	onamae wa
My name is…	…です。
	…desu
Pleased to meet you.	よろしくお願いします。
	yoroshiku onegai shimasu
Where are you from?	どちらからですか。
	dochira kara desu ka

I'm from the U.S./U.K.	アメリカ/イギリスからです。
	amerika/igirisu kara desu
What do you do?	何をしていますか。
	nani o shite imasu ka
I work for…	…に勤めています。
	…ni tsutomete imasu
I'm a student.	学生です。
	gakusee desu
I'm retired.	退職しました。
	taishoku shimashita
Do you like…?	は好きですか。
	…wa suki desu ka
Goodbye.	さようなら。
	sayoonara
See you later.	それではまた。
	sore dewa mata

LANGUAGE DIFFICULTIES

Do you speak English?	英語ができますか
	eego ga dekimasu ka
Does anyone here speak English?	英語ができる人はいますか。
	eego ga dekiru hito wa imasu ka
I don't speak (much) Japanese.	(あまり) 日本語ができません。
	(amari) nihongo ga dekimasen
Could you speak more slowly?	ゆっくり言ってくれませんか。
	yukkuri itte kuremasen ka
Could you repeat that?	もう一度、言ってくれませんか。
	moo ichido itte kuremasen ka
Excuse me? [Pardon?]	すみません
	sumimasen

What was that?	何ですか。
	nan desu ka
Please write it down.	書いてください。
	kaite kudasai
Can you translate this for me?	訳してください。
	yakushite kudasai
What does this/that mean?	これ/それは、何という意味ですか。
	kore/sore wa nan to yuu imi desu ka
I understand.	分力、りました。
	wakarimashita
I don't understand.	分かりません。
	wakarimasen
Do you understand?	分力、り・ます力、。
	wakarimasu ka

It is customary in Japan to address people by their last name first, though more recently when meeting foreigners many Japanese will give their surname last. Generally, the suffix-**san** (Mr., Mrs., or Ms.) is used after the last name, so someone with a last name of Honda and a first name of Kenji would be addressed as Honda-**san**. Never use **san** to talk about yourself.

MAKING FRIENDS

Hello.	こんにちは
	konnichi wa
Pleased to meet you!	初めまして。
	hajimemashite
Good morning.	おはようございます。
	ohayoo gozaimasu

English	Japanese	Romaji
Good afternoon.	こんにちは。	*konnichi wa*
Good evening.	こんばんは。	*konban wa*
My name is...	…です。	*...desu*
What's your name?	お名前は。	*onamae wa*
I'd like to introduce you to...	…さんをご紹介します	*...san o goshookai shimasu*
Nice to meet you.	よろしくお願いします。	*yoroshiku onegai shimasu*
How are you?	お元気ですか。	*ogenki desu ka*
Fine, thanks.	はい、おかげさまで。	*hai, okage sama de.*
And you?	いかがですか。	*ikaga desu ka*

Japanese has three levels of speech: plain, polite and honorific. Which level to use is determined by how well you know the other person, and also by age, social status and situation. Female speakers tend to employ polite speech, and young people often use plain speech. Japanese culture emphasizes respect, so honorific speech is appropriate when a younger person addresses an older person, or a person in an organization or company addresses a superior. Honorific speech is also used when trying to sell goods or services to others.

An appropriate greeting for the first meeting between adults is **Hajimemashite**, which literally means 'For the first time'. In subsequent meetings, this changes to **konnichi wa** (during the day) or **konban wa** (in the afternoon), which are still polite. **Yaa** (for men) and **Ara** (for women), both meaning Hi! are only appropriate among friends, in a casual setting. In this book, you will find polite and honorific speech style.

YOU MAY SEE...

英語が少ししかできません。 *eego ga sukoshi shika dekimasen*	I only speak a little English.
英語はできません。 *eego wa dekimasen*	I don't speak English.

TRAVEL TALK

I'm here...	…で来ました。
	...dekimashita
on business	仕事
	shigoto
on vacation [holiday]	観光 [休暇]
	kankoo [kyuuka]
studying	研究
	kenkyuu
I'm staying for...	…間、滞在しています。
	...kan taizai shiteimasu
I've been here...	…前に、来ました。
	...mae ni kimashita
a day	日
	nichi/hi
a week	週
	shuu
a month	月
	tsuki
Where are you from?	どちらからですか。
	dochira kara desu ka
I'm from...	…から来ました。
	...kara kimashita

For Numbers, see page 20.

PERSONAL

Who are you with?	どなたとご一緒ですか。
	donata to goissho desu ka
I'm on my own.	一人です。
	hitori desu

I'm with my...	…と一緒です。
	…to issho desu
husband/wife	主人/家内
	shujin/kanai
boyfriend/ girlfriend	ボーイフレンド/ガールフレンド
	booifurendo/gaarufurendo
friend(s)	友人
	yuujin
colleague(s)	同僚
	dooryoo
When's your birthday?	誕生日はいつですか。
	tanjoobi wa itsu desu ka
How old are you?	何歳ですか。
	nansai desu ka
I'm...	…歳です。
	…sai desu
Are you married?	結婚していますか。
	kekkon shite imasu ka
I'm...	私は…
	watashi wa…
single	ひとりです。
	hitori desu
in a relationship	付き合っています。
	tsukiatte imasu

engaged	…婚約中です。
	kon-yaku chuu desu
married	結婚しています。
	kekkon shite imasu
divorced	離婚しました。
	rikon shimashita
separated	別居中です。
	bekkyo chuu desu
I'm widowed.	妻/夫を亡くしました。
	tsuma f/otto m o nakushimashita
Do you have children/ grandchildren?	お子さん/お孫さんがいますか。
	okosan/omagosan ga imasu ka

WORK & SCHOOL

What do you do?	(お仕事は)何をしていますか。
	(oshigoto wa)nani o shite imasu ka
What are you studying?	何を勉強していますか。
	nani o benkyoo shite imasu ka
I'm studying…	…を勉強しています。
	…o benkyoo shite imasu
I work full time/part time.	フルタイム/パートタイムです。
	furu/paato taimu desu
I'm between jobs.	求職中です。
	kyuushoku chuu desu
I work at home.	自宅で仕事をしています。
	jitaku de shigoto o shiteimasu
Who do you work for?	どちらにお勤めですか。
	dochira ni otsutome desu ka
I work for…	…に勤めています。
	…ni tsutomete imasu
Here's my business card.	名刺をどうぞ。
	meeshi o doozo

WEATHER

What's the weather forecast for tomorrow?	明日の予報は何ですか。 *ashita no yohoo wa nan desu ka*
What beautiful/terrible weather!	なんてきれいな/いやな天気なんでしょう。 *nante kireina/iyana tenki nan deshoo*
It's cool/warm.	涼しい/暖かいです。 *suzushii/atatakai desu*
It's rainy/sunny.	雨/晴れです。 *ame/hare desu*
It's snowy/icy.	雪が降って/凍っています。 *yuki ga futte/kootte imasu*
Do I need a jacket/an umbrella?	上着/傘がいりますか。 *uwagi/kasa ga irimasu ka*

ON THE WAY

GETTING AROUND

NEED TO KNOW

How do I get to town?	どうしたら町に行けますか。
	dooshitara machi ni ikemasu ka
How far is it?	距離はどのくらいですか。
	kyori wa dono kurai desu ka
Where can I buy tickets?	切符はどこで買えますか。
	kippu wa doko de kaemasu ka
Where's…?	…はどこですか。
	…wa doko desu ka
the airport	空港
	kuukoo
the train station	駅
	eki
the bus station	バスターミナル
	basu taaminaru
the subway [underground] station	地下鉄の駅
	chikatetsu no eki

A one-way [single]/ round-trip [return] ticket.	片道/往復 *katamichi/oofuku*
How much?	いくらですか。 *ikura desuka*
Are there any discounts?	割引料金はありますか。 *waribiki ryookin wa arimasu ka*
Which…?	どちらの *… dochira no…*
gate	ゲート *geeto*
line	線 *sen*
platform	ホーム *hoomu*
Where can I get a taxi?	タクシーはどこで乗れますか。 *takushii wa doko de noremasu ka*
Please take me to this address.	この住所までお願いします。 *konojuusho made onegai shimasu*
Where can I rent a car?	レンタカーはどこで借りられますか。 *rentakaa wa doko de kariraremasu ka*
Can I have a map?	地図をお願いします。 *chizu o onegai shimasu*

TICKETS

When's…to Kyoto?	京都行きの…は何時ですか。 *kyootoikino…wa nanji desu ka*
the (first) bus	(始発)バス *(shihatsu) basu*
the (next) flight	(次の)便 *(tsugi no) bin*

the last train	終電
	shuuden
Where can I buy tickets?	切符はどこで買えますか。
	kippu wa doko de kaemasu ka
One/Two ticket(s), please.	切符一枚/二枚お願いします。
	kippu ichimai/nimai onegai shimasu
For today/tomorrow.	今日/あしたの
	kyoo/ashita no
A...ticket	…チケット
	...chiketto
one-way [single]	片道
	katamichi
round-trip [return]	往復
	oofuku
first class	ファーストクラス
	faasuto kurasu
business class	ビジネス・クラス
	bijinesu kurasu
economy class	エコノミー
	ekonomii
How much?	いくらですか。
	ikura desuka
Is there a discount for...?	…割引はありますか。
	...waribiki wa arimasu ka
children	子供の
	kodomo no
students	学生
	gakusee
senior citizens	高齢者
	kooreesha
tourists	観光客向けの
	kankookyaku mukeno
The express bus/ express train, please.	高速バス/特急電車をお願いします。
	koosoku basu/tokkyuu densha o onegai shimasu

The local bus/ train, please.	**路線バス/普通電車をお願いします。** *rosen basu/futsuu densha o onegai shimasu*
I have an e-ticket.	**Eチケットがあります。** *iichiketto ga arimasu*
Can I buy a ticket on the bus/train?	**バス/電車 の中で切符が買えますか。** *basu/densha no nakade kippu ga kaemasu ka*
I'd like to…my reservation.	**予約を…したいんですが。** *yoyaku o …shitian desu ga*
cancel	**キャンセル** *kyanseru*
change	**変更** *henkoo*
confirm	**確認** *kakunin*

For Days, see page 26.

AIRPORT TRANSFER

How much is a taxi to the airport?	**空港までタクシーはいくらですか。** *kuukoo made takushii wa ikura desu ka*
To…Airport, please.	**…空港までお願いします。** *…kuukoo made onegai shimasu*
My airline is…	**航空会社は…です。** *kookuu gaisha wa…desu*
My flight leaves at…	**飛行機の便は…に出ます。** *hikooki no bin wa… ni demasu*
I'm in a rush.	**急いでいます 。** *isoide imasu*
Can you take an alternate route?	**他の道を行ってください。** *hoka no michi o itte kudasai*

Can you drive faster/ slower?

もっとはやく/ゆっくり 運転してくれません か。

motto hayaku/yukkuri unten shite kuremasenka

YOU MAY HEAR...

どの航空会社をご利用ですか。
dono kookuu gaisha o goriyoo desu ka
国内線ですか,国際線ですか。
kokunaisen desu ka kokusaisen desu ka
どのターミナルですか。
dono taaminaru desu ka

What airline are you flying?
Domestic or International?
What terminal?

YOU MAY SEE...

到着 *toochaku*	arrivals
出発 *shuppatsu*	departures
荷物引渡場 *nimotsu hikiwatashijoo*	baggage claim
国内線 *kokunaisen*	domestic flights
国際線 *kokusaisen*	international flights
チェックインデスク *chekku in desuku*	check-in desk
Eチケットチェックイン *e-chiketto chekku in*	e-ticket check-in
出発ゲート *shuppatsu geeto*	departure gates

CHECKING IN

Where is the check-in desk for flight...?	…便のチェックインデスクはどこですか。 *…bin no chekkuin desuku wa doko desu ka*
My name is...	…です。 *…desu*
I'm going to...	…へ行きます。 *…e ikimasu*
How much luggage is allowed?	荷物はどれくらい持ち込めますか。 *nimotsu wa dore kurai mochikomemasu ka*
Which gate does flight... leave from?	…便のゲートは何番ですか。 *… bin no geeto wa nanban desu ka*
I'd like a window/an aisle seat.	窓側/通路側の席をお願いします。 *madogawa/tsuurogawa no seki o onegaishimasu*
When do we leave/arrive?	何時に出ますか/着きますか。 *nanji ni demasu ka/tsukimasu ka*
Is flight...delayed?	…便は遅れていますか。 *…bin wa okurete imasu ka*
How late will it be?	どのくらい遅れますか。 *dono kurai okuremasu ka*

YOU MAY HEAR...

次の方
tsugi no kata

Next!

チケット/パスポートをお見せください。
chiketto/pasupooto o omise kudasai

Your ticket/
passport,
please.

お荷物はいくつありますか。
onimotsu wa ikutsu arimasu ka

How many
pieces of
luggage do you
have?

重量超過です。
juuryoo chooka desu

You have
excess
baggage.

**それは手荷物には重すぎます/
大きすぎます。**
*sore wa tenimostu ni wa omosugimasu/
ookisugimasu*

That's too
heavy/large for
a carry-on
[to carry on
board].

お荷物は、ご自分で詰められましたか。
*onimotsu wa gojibun de tsumeraremashita
ka*

Did you pack
these bags
yourself?

誰かに何か運ぶように頼まれましたか。
*dareka ni nanika hakobuyooni
tanomaremashita ka*

Did anyone
give you
anything to
carry?

ポケットのものを出してください。
poketto no mono o dashite kudasai

Empty your
pockets.

靴を脱いでください。
kutsu o nuide kudasai

Take off your
shoes.

…便のお客様はご搭乗いただきます。
*…bin no okyakusama wa gotoojoo
itadakimasu*

Now boarding
flight…

LUGGAGE

Where is/are the...? …はどこですか。
...wa doko desu ka

luggage carts [trolleys]	カート *kaato*
luggage lockers	コインロッカー *koin rokkaa*
baggage claim	荷物引渡場 *nimotsu hikiwatashijoo*

My luggage has been lost.
荷物がなくなりました。
nimotsu ga nakunarimashita

My luggage has been stolen.
荷物が盗まれました。
nimotsu ga nusumaremashita

My suitcase was damaged.
スーツケースが壊れています。
suutsukeesu ga kowarete imasu

A Travel Help Line is run by the Japan National Tourist Organization (JNTO). An English-speaking travel expert is available. Ask at your hotel or at a tourist information center for the phone number.

FINDING YOUR WAY

Where is/are the...? …はどこですか。
...wa doko desu ka

currency exchange office	両替所 *ryoogaejo*
car rental [hire]	レンタカー *rentakaa*

Where is/are the...?	…はどこですか。
	...wa doko desu ka
exit	出口
	deguchi
taxis	タクシー
	takushii
Is there a...into town?	町に行く…はありますか。
	machi ni iku ...wa arimasu ka
bus	バス
	basu
train	電車
	densha
subway	地下鉄
	chikatetsu

For Asking Directions, see page 65.

TRAIN

How do I get to the train station?	駅には、どうやって行けますか。
	eki niwa doo yatte ikemasu ka
How far is it?	距離はどのくらいですか 。
	kyori wa dono kurai desu ka
Where is/are the...?	…はどこですか。
	...wa doko desu ka
ticket office	きっぷうりば
	kippu uriba
information desk	受付
	uketsuke
luggage lockers	コインロッカー
	koin rokkaa
platforms	ホーム
	hoomu

Can I have a schedule [timetable]?	時刻表をください。
	jikokuhyoo o kudasai
How long is the trip?	どのくらいかかりますか。
	dono kurai kakarimasu ka
Is it a direct train?	この電車は直行便ですか。
	kono densha wa chokkoobin desu ka
Do I have to change trains?	乗り換えはありますか。
	norikae wa arimasu ka
Is the train on time?	電車は時間通りですか。
	densya wa jikandoori desu ka

For Time, see page 25.

YOU MAY SEE...

ホーム	platforms
案内係	information
予約窓口	reservations
到着	arrivals
出発	departures

Japan's rail network covers the whole country. There are many different rail operators, and the service is clean, safe, and punctual. First-class cars are called **guriin sha** (green cars) and are marked with a green four-leaf sign. To travel first class you need a special ticket in addition to the normal ticket. Second-class cars have reserved seats and unreserved seats. Reserved seats are a little more expensive. The types of train are:

新幹線 **shinkansen**, the bullet train. This is the fastest rail service. There are lines in Honshu (main island), Kyushu (south island), and Hokkaido (north island). There are three types: **Nozomi** (the fastest train), **Hikari** and **Kodama**.

特急 **tokkyuu**, limited express. This service is for long-distance travel.

急行 **kyuuko**, the ordinary medium-distance express.

快速 **kaisoku**, rapid train. This commuter service has no surcharge above the basic fare.

普通 **futsuu**, local train. This commuter service has no surcharge above the basic fare.

Tourists can buy special passes for unlimited travel on the rail system, as well as on buses and ferries, throughout Japan. These passes must be bought outside Japan, from offices of Japan Air Lines, travel agents, or Japan Travel Bureau offices. There are a number of other special discounts for travel along certain lines within designated areas over a set period, for example **Shuuyuuken** (周遊券), **Free kippu** (フリーきっぷ), and **Parent-Child Super Pass** (親子スーパーパス). Enquire about these tickets at station travel shops.

Most tickets are bought from vending machines. Find your destination on the diagram above the machines, insert money (change is given), and press the button for the appropriate amount. The station names on the diagram are usually in Japanese only, so it is important to know the characters of the station you are going to.

DEPARTURES

Which track [platform] for the train to…?	…行きの列車は何番ホームですか。 *…iki no ressha wa nan-ban hoomu desu ka*
Is this the track [platform] to…?	…行きのホームはここですか。 *… iki no hoomu wa koko desu ka*
Where is track [platform]…?	…行きのホームはどこですか。 *… iki no hoomu wa doko desu ka*
Where do I change for…?	…へ行くには、どこで乗り換えますか。 *…e ikuniwa doko de norikaemasu ka*

YOU MAY HEAR…

ご乗車の方はお急ぎください。 *gojoosha no kata wa oisogi kudasai*	All aboard!
乗車券を拝見します。 *jooshaken o haiken shimasu*	Tickets, please.
…で乗り換えてください。 *…de norikaete kudasai*	You have to change at…
次の停車駅は *…tsugi no teishaeki wa …*	Next stop…

ON BOARD

Can I sit here?	ここに座ってもいいですか。 *koko ni suwattemo iidesuka*
Can I open the window?	窓を開けてもいいですか。 *mado o aketemo iidesu ka*
Is this seat taken?	この席は空いていますか。 *kono seki wa aite imasu ka*

That's my seat.	そこは私の席です。
	soko wa watashi no seki desu
Here's my reservation.	こちらが予約票です。
	kochira ga yoyakuhyoo desu

BUS

Where's the bus station?	バスのターミナルはどこですか。
	basu no taaminaru wa doko desu ka
How far is it?	距離はどのくらいですか 。
	kyori wa dono kurai desu ka
How do I get to...?	どうしたら…に行けますか。
	dooshitara...ni ikemasu ka
Does the bus stop at...?	…に止まりますか。
	...ni tomarimasu ka
Could you tell me when to get off?	下りる場所が来たら、教えてください 。
	oriru basho ga kitara oshiete kudasai
Do I have to change buses?	乗り換えはありますか。
	norikae wa arimasu ka
Stop here, please!	ここで止めてください。
	kokode tomete kudasai

For Tickets, see page 47.

There are extensive city and rural bus services in Japan. Some towns, such as Hakone, Nagasaki and Kumamoto, have streetcars [trams]. When you board a bus take a numbered ticket and pay at the end. You can save money by buying **kaisuuken**, multiple-ride tickets.

YOU MAY SEE...

バス停留所/バス停	bus stop
入口/出口	enter/exit

SUBWAY

Where's the nearest Subway station?	最寄りの地下鉄の駅はどこですか。
	moyori no chikatetsu no eki wa doko desu ka
Could I have a map of the subway, please?	地下鉄の路線図をください。
	chikatetsu no rosenzu o kudasai
Which line for...?	…は、何線ですか。
	...wa nanisen desu ka
Which direction?	どこ行きですか。
	doko iki desu ka
Do I have to transfer [change]?	乗り換えが必要ですか。
	norikae ga hitsuyoo desu ka
Is this the subway [train] to...?	この電車は …へ行きますか。
	kono densha wa...e ikimasu ka

Tokyo, Osaka, Nagoya and other big cities have very efficient subway systems. A map showing the various lines and stations is displayed outside **chikatetsu**, subway stations. Trains are frequent and run until around midnight. Station platform signs are in Japanese and English. Avoid rush hours (7:00 - 9:00 a.m. and 5:00 - 7:00 p.m.), when trains can be extremely crowded.

How many stops to...?	…までの停車駅はいくつですか。
	… made no teesya eki wa ikutsu desu ka
Where are we?	ここは、どこですか。
	koko wa doko desu ka

BOAT & FERRY

When is the car ferry to Okinawa?	沖縄行きのカーフェリーは、何時ですか。
	okinawa iki no kaa ferii wa nanji desu ka
What time is the **next** sailing?	次の出航は何時ですか。
	tsugi no syukkoo wa nanji desu ka
Can I book a seat/cabin?	座席/船室を予約したいんですが。
	zaseki/senshitsu o yoyaku shitain desu ga
How long is the crossing?	到着までどのくらいかかりますか。
	toochaku made dono kurai kakarimasu ka

For Tickets, see page 47.

Ferry services run from Honshu (the main island) to the other islands. Details about ports and sailings may be obtained from the Tourist Information Center (TIC). To sample the charms of the Inland Sea, travel by ferry or hydrofoil is recommended.

Various cruises are available in the Tokyo Bay area, many departing from Hinode Pier (日の出桟橋 **hinode sanbashi**). In Kobe, travelers may enjoy 50-minute port cruises departing from Naka Pier. In Yokohama, you can find 50-minute tours of the harbor leaving from near the retired cruise liner, Hikawa Maru.

TAXI

Where can I get a taxi?	タクシーはどこで乗れますか。 *takushii wa doko de noremasu ka*
I'd like a taxi now/for tomorrow.	今/明日 タクシーをお願いします。 *ima/ashita takushii o onegai shimasu*
Do you have the number for a taxi?	タクシー会社の電話番号をご存知ですか。 *takushii gaisha no denwa bangoo o gozonji desu ka*
Can you send a taxi?	タクシーを呼んでもらえますか。 *takushii o yonde morae masu ka*
Pick me up at (place/time).	(place)に/(time)に来てください。 *...ni kite kudasai*
I'm going to...	⋯へ行きます。 *...e ikimasu*
this address	この住所 *kono juusho*
the airport	空港 *kuukoo*
the train [railway] station	駅 *eki*
I'm late.	急いでいるんです。 *isoide irun desu*
Can you drive faster/slower?	急いで/ゆっくり運転してください。 *isoide/yukkuri unten shite kudasai*

YOU MAY HEAR...

どちらまで。 *dochira made*	Where to?
ご住所は。 *gojuusho wa*	What's the address?

Stop/Wait here.	ここで止めて/待っていてください。 *kokode tomete/matteite kudasai*
How much?	いくらですか。 *ikura desuka*
You said it would cost…yen.	…円ですね。 *…en desu ne*
Keep the change.	お釣りは結構です。 *otsuri wa kekkoo desu*
A receipt, please.	レシートをお願いします。 *reshiito o onegai shimasu*

Taxis are usually yellow or green. If the light in the bottom right-hand corner of the windshield is red, the taxi is free; if it's green, it's occupied. The rear doors are remote controlled — be careful not to get knocked over by them! Few taxi drivers speak English, so have your destination written down on paper. Taxi drivers do not expect to be tipped.

BICYCLE & MOTORBIKE

I'd like to rent…	…を借りたいんですが。 *…o karitain desu ga*
a 3-/10-speed bicycle	3速/10速の自転車 *sansoku/jussoku no jitensha*
a moped	スクーター *sukuutaa*
a motorcycle	オートバイ *ootobai*
How much per day/week?	一日/一週間、いくらですか。いくらですか。 *ichinichi/isshuukan ikura desu ka*

Can I have a helmet/ lock? — ヘルメット/ロックをお願いします。
herumetto/rokku o onegai shimasu

I have a puncture/ flat tyre. — タイヤがパンクしています。
taiya ga panku shite imasu

CAR HIRE

Where can I rent a car? — レンタカーはどこで借りられますか。
rentakaa wa doko de kariraremasu ka

I'd like to rent... — …を借りたいんですが。
...o karitain desu ga

  a 2-/4-door car — 2/4ドア車
tsuu/foo doa sha

  an automatic — オートマチック
ootomachikku

  a car with air conditioning — エアコン付の車
eakon tsuki no kuruma

  a car seat — チャイルドシート
chairudo shiito

How much...? — いくら
ikura

  per day/week — 一日/一週間
ichinichi/isshuukan

  per kilometer — 一キロ
ichi kiro

  for unlimited mileage — 距離は無制限で
kyori wa museigen de

  with insurance — 保険付きで
hoken tsuki de

Are there any special weekend rates? — 週末料金はありますか。
shuumatsu ryookin wa arimasu ka

(Where's) the parking meter? — パーキングメーター（はどこですか。）
paakingu meetaa (wa doko desu ka)

YOU MAY HEAR...

国際免許証をお持ちですか。
kokusai menkyoshoo o omochi desu ka

Do you have an international driver's license?

パスポートをお見せください。
pasupooto o omise kudasai

Your passport, please.

保険をお掛けになりますか。
hoken o okakeni narimasu ka

Do you want insurance?

…の前金をいただきます。
…no maekin o itadakimasu

There is a deposit of…

ここにサインをお願いします。
koko ni sain o onegai shimasu

Please sign here.

(Where's...) the parking garage?

駐車場 (はどこですか。)
chuushajoo (wa doko desu ka)

FUEL STATION

Where's the fuel station?	ガソリンスタンドはどこですか。 *gasorin sutando wa doko desu ka*
Fill it up, please.	満タンにしてください。 *mantan ni shite kudasai*
...liters, please.	…リットルお願いします。 *...rittoru onegai shimasu*
I'll pay in cash/by credit card.	現金/(クレジット)カードで払います。 *genkin/(kurejitto) kaado de haraimasu*

YOU MAY SEE...

レギュラー	regular
スーパー	premium [super]
ディーゼル	diesel

ASKING DIRECTIONS

Is this the right road to...?	…に行くのは、この道でいいんですか。 *...ni ikuno wa kono michi de iin desu ka*
How far is it to...?	…まで、どのくらいありますか。 *...made donokurai arimasu ka*
Where's...?	…はどこですか。 *...wa doko desu ka*
...Street	…通り *...doori*
this address	この住所 *kono juusho*
the highway [motorway]	高速道路 *koosoku dooro*

Can you show me on
the map?

I'm lost.

この地図で教えてください。
kono chizu de oshiete kudasai

道に迷いました。
michi ni mayoimashita

YOU MAY HEAR...

まっすぐ *massugu*	straight ahead
左 *hidari*	left
右 *migi*	right
角/道を曲がったところ *kado/michi o magatta tokoro*	on/around the corner
向かい *mukai*	across
後ろ *ushiro*	behind
のとなり *no tonari*	next to
北/南 *kita/minami*	north/south
東/西 *higashi/nishi*	east/west
信号 *shingoo*	traffic light
交差点 *koosaten*	intersection

YOU MAY SEE...

	stop		slow down
	minimum speed		time-limited parking
	no standing		no parking
	dangerous curve		one way
	no entry		

PARKING

Can I park here?	ここに駐車してもいいですか。 *koko ni chuusha shitemo ii desu ka*
Where is the nearest parking garage?	この近くに駐車場はありますか。 *kono chikaku ni chuushajoo wa arimasu ka*
How much...?	…いくらですか。 *...ikura desuka*
per hour	一時間 *ichijikan*
per day	一日 *ichinichi*
overnight	一晩 *hitoban*
(Where's the) the parking meter?	パーキングメーター（はどこですか。） *paakingu meetaa (wa doko desu ka)*

Street parking is limited. It is common to have your
car towed away or booted if you park in illegal spaces. It is
an expensive and time-consuming process to get it back.
Some hotels have parking facilities, otherwise the best
solution is to use designated parking garages.

BREAKDOWN & REPAIR

My car broke down/ won't start.	車が壊れました。/スタートしません。 *kuruma ga kowaremashita/sutaato shimasen*
Can you fix it?	直してもらえませんか。 *naoshite moraemasen ka*
When will it be ready?	いつ直りますか。 *itsu naorimasu ka*
How much?	いくらですか。 *ikura desuka*
I have a puncture/ flat tyre.	タイヤがパンクしています。 *taiya ga panku shite imasu*

ACCIDENTS

There has been an accident.	事故がありました。 *jiko ga arimashita*
Call an ambulance/ the police.	警察/救急車を呼んでください。 *keesatsu/kyuukyuusha o yonde kudasai*

PLACES TO STAY

NEED TO KNOW

Can you recommend a hotel in…?	…で良いホテルを教えてください。
	…de ii hoteru o oshiete kudasai
I have a reservation.	予約してあります。
	yoyaku shite arimasu
My name is…	…です。
	…desu
Do you have a room…?	…部屋はありますか。
	…heya wa arimasu ka
with a bathroom	バス付きの
	basu tsuki no
with AC	エアコン付きの
	eakon tsuki no
Do you have a room for one/two?	一人/二人部屋はありますか。
	hitori/futari beya wa arimasuka
For tonight	今晩
	konban

For two nights	二晩
	futaban
For one week	一週間
	isshuukan
How much?	いくらですか。
	ikura desuka
Is there anything cheaper?	もっと安い部屋はありますか。
	motto yasui heya wa arimasu ka
When's check-out?	チェックアウトは何時ですか。
	chekkuautowa nanji desu ka
Can I leave this in the safe?	これを金庫に預けたいんですが。
	kore o kinko ni azuketain desu ga
Can I leave my bags?	荷物を預けたいんですが。
	nimotsu o azuketain desu ga
Can I have the bill/a receipt?	レシート/会計をお願いします。
	kaikee/reshiito o onegai shimasu
I'll pay in cash/by credit card.	現金/(クレジット)カードで払います。
	genkin/(kurejitto) kaado de haraimasu

SOMEWHERE TO STAY

Can you recommend a hotel?	いホテルを教えてください。
	iihoteruooshiete kudasai
Can you recommend a capsule hotel?	どこか良いカプセルホテルはありますか。
	dokoka yoi kapuseru hoteru wa arimasu ka
Can you recommend a hostel?	どこか良い ホステル はありますか。
	dokoka yoi hosuteru wa arimasu ka
Can you recommend a campsite?	どこか良い キャンプ場 はありますか 。
	dokoka yoi kyanpujoo wa arimasu ka
Can you recommend a bed and breakfast?	どこか良い民宿 はありますか 。
	dokoka yoi minsyuku wa arimasu ka

Can you recommend an inn?	どこか良い旅館はありますか。 *dokoka yoi ryokan wa arimasu ka*
What is it near?	どこの近くですか。 *doko no chikaku desu ka*
How do I get there?	どうやって行くんですか。 *dooyatte ikun desu ka*

There are many different places to stay in Japan.
ホテル **hoteru** are Western-style hotels. These are
comparable to western hotels.
ビジネスホテル **bijinesu hoteru**, or business hotels, have
small rooms, often with no room service. They are clean
and comfortable and usually located near train stations.
旅館 **ryokan** are Japanese-style inns. For a taste of the
Japanese way of life, a stay at a **ryokan** is recommended.
Many are situated in beautiful settings with access to hot
springs. Room prices include breakfast, dinner, and service
charge. The majority offer only traditional style bathrooms,
meals and sleeping arrangements.
Another good way of sampling authentic Japanese lodgings
is a 民宿 **minshuku**, or guest house. **Minshuku** are often
family run and have an informal, friendly atmosphere. The
overnight charge includes dinner and breakfast.
For those with a particular interest in Buddhism, 宿防
shukuboo, temple accommodation, will allow you to join in
the monks' daily life.

AT THE HOTEL

I have a reservation.	予約してあります。 *yoyaku shite arimasu*

My name is…	…です。 *…desu*
Do you have a room…?	…部屋はありますか。 *…heya wa arimasu ka*
with a bathroom [toilet]/shower	バス/シャワー付きの *basu/shawaa tukino*
with AC	エアコンつきの *eakon tsuki no*
that's smoking/non-smoking	喫煙/禁煙の *kitsuen/kinen no*
for tonight	今晩 *konban*
for two nights	二晩 *futaban*
for one week	一週間 *isshuukan*
Does the hotel have…?	ホテルに…はありますか。 *hoteru ni… wa arimasu ka*
a computer	コンピュータ *konpyuuta*
an elevator [lift]	エレベーター *erebeetaa*
(wireless) internet service	(ワイアレス)インターネットサービス *(waiaresu) intaanetto saabisu*
room service	ルームサービス *ruumu saabisu*
a gym	フィットネスセンター *fittonesu sentaa*
a pool	プール *puuru*
I need…	…が要るんですが。 *…ga irun desu ga*
an extra bed	もう一つベッド *moo hitotsu beddo*

a cot	折り畳みベッド
	oritatami beddo
a crib [child's cot]	ベビーベッド
	bebii beddo

YOU MAY HEAR...

パスポート/カードをお願いします。	Your passport/
pasupooto/kaado o onegai shimasu	credit card
	please.
この用紙にご記入ください。	Please fill out
kono yooshi ni gokinyuu kudasai	this form.
ここにサインをお願いします。	Sign here.
koko ni sain o onegai shimasu	

PRICE

How much per night/ week?	一泊/一週間いくらですか。
	ippaku/isshuukan ikura desu ka
Does the price include breakfast/ sales tax [VAT]?	この料金は朝食/消費税込みですか。
	kono ryookin wa chooshoku/shoohi zee komi desu ka

PREFERENCES

Can I see the room?	部屋を見せてもらえますか。
	heya o misete morae masu ka
I'd like a...room.	…部屋にしてもらえますか。
	...heya ni shite morae masu ka
better	もっと良い
	motto yoi

bigger	もっと大きい
	motto ookii
cheaper	もっと安い
	motto yasui
quieter	もっと静かな
	motto shizuka na
I'll take it.	それにします。
	sore ni shimasu
No, I won't take it.	いいえ、結構です。
	Iie kekkou desu

QUESTIONS

Where's the...?	…はどこですか。
	...wa doko desu ka
bar	バー
	baa
bathroom [toilet]	トイレ
	toire
elevator [lift]	エレベーター
	erebeetaa
Can I have...?	…をお願いします。
	...o onegai shimasu
a blanket	毛布
	moofu
an iron	アイロン
	airon
the room key	ルームキー
	ruumu kii
key card	キーカード
	kii kaado
a pillow	枕
	makura

soap	石鹸
	sekken
toilet paper	トイレットペーパー
	toiretto peepaa
a towel	タオル
	taoru
Do you have an adapter for this?	アダプタはありますか。
	adaputa wa arimasu ka
How do I turn on the lights?	電気はどうやって付けますか。
	denki wa dooyatte tsukemasu ka
Could you wake me at…?	…時に起こしてください。
	…ji ni okoshite kudasai
Can I leave this in the safe?	これを金庫に保管できますか。
	kore o kinko ni hokan dekimasu ka
Could I have my things from the safe?	私のものを金庫から出してください。
	watashi no mono o kinko kara dashite kudasai
Is/are there any mail/messages for me?	手紙/メッセージがありますか。
	tegami/messeeji ga arimasu ka
Do you have a laundry service?	ランドリーサービスはありますか。
	randorii saabisu wa arimasu ka

There are two types of toilet you may find in Japan.
Traditional Japanese squat toilets have nothing to
sit down on, and the user squats down to use the facility.
These toilets flush just like western style. You will also find
some toilets like you see in the West. Western style toilets
may range from very basic to a high-tech model which will
have a heated seat, water jets to wash and warm air to dry,
and an automatic mechanism to flush and close the lid.

👁

YOU MAY SEE...

押す/引く	push/pull
トイレ	restroom [toilet]
シャワー	shower
エレベーター	elevator [lift]
階段	stairs
洗濯室	laundry
起こさないでください	do not disturb
防火扉	fire door
非常口	(emergency) exit
モーニングコール	wake-up call

PROBLEMS

There's a problem.	ちょっと困っているんですが。 *chotto komatte irun desu ga*
I've lost my key/key card.	鍵/カードキーをなくしました。 *kagi/kaado kii o nakushimashita*
I've locked myself out of my room.	鍵を部屋に置いたまま出てきてしまいました。 *kagi o heya ni oitamama detekite shimaimashita*
There's no hot water/toilet paper.	お湯/トイレットペーパーがないんですが。 *oyu/toiretto peepaa ga nain desuga*
The room is dirty.	部屋が汚いんですが。 *heya ga kitanain desu ga*
There are bugs in our room.	部屋に虫がいるんですが。 *heya ni mushi ga irun desuga*
The...has broken down.	…が壊れたんですが。 *...ga kowaretan desuga*

Can you fix...?	…を直してもらえますか。
	…o naoshite moraemasu ka
the AC	エアコン
	eakon
the fan	扇風機
	senpuuki
the heat [heating]	暖房
	danboo
the light	電気
	denki
the TV	テレビ
	terebi
the toilet	トイレ
	toire
I'd like to move to another room.	部屋を替えてください。
	heya o kaete kudasai

Japan uses the 100 volt electricity system. You may need a converter and/or adapter for your appliances.

CHECKING OUT

When's check-out?	チェックアウトは何時ですか。 *chekkuauto wa nanji desu ka*
Could I leave my bags here until…?	…まで荷物を置いておいてもいいですか。 *…made nimotsu o oite oitemo ii desu ka*
Can I have an itemized bill/a receipt?	明細書/レシートをお願いします。 *meesaisho/reshiito o onegai shimasu*
I think there's a mistake in this bill.	この会計は違っているようですが。 *kono kaikee wa chigatte iru yoo desu ga*
I'll pay in cash/by credit card.	現金/(クレジット)カードで払います。 *genkin/(kurejitto) kaado de haraimasu*

Tipping isn't customary and is officially discouraged. Porters at airports and train stations charge a set fee. Hotels, **ryokan** (Japanese inns) and restaurants add a 10-15% service charge to the bill.

RENTING

I've reserved an apartment/a room.	アパート/部屋を借りました。 *apaato/heya o karimashita*
My name is…	…です。 *…desu*
Can I have the key/key card?	鍵/カードキーをお願いします。 *kagi/kaado kii o onegai shimasu*
Are there…?	…はありますか *…wa arimasu ka*
dishes and utensils	食器 *shokki*

pillows	枕
	makura
Are there...?	…はありますか 。
	...wa arimasu ka
sheets	シーツ
	shiitsu
towels	タオル
	taoru
When/Where do I put out the trash [rubbish]?	ゴミはどこへ/いつ出すんですか。
	gomi wa doko e/itsu dasun desu ka
...is broken.	…が壊れているんですが。
	...ga kowarete irun desuga
How does...work?	…はどうやって使えばいいんですか。
	...wa dooyatte tsukaeba ii n desu ka
the air-conditioner	エアコン
	eakon
the dishwasher	食洗機
	shokusen ki
the freezer	冷凍庫
	reetooko
the heater	ヒーター
	hiitaa
the microwave	電子レンジ
	denshi renji
the refrigerator	冷蔵庫
	reezooko
the stove	コンロ
	konro
the washing machine	洗濯機
	sentakuki

DOMESTIC ITEMS

I need…	…が要るんですが。
	…ga irun desu ga
an adapter	アダプタ
	adaputa
aluminum [kitchen] foil	アルミホイル
	arumi hoiru
a bottle opener	栓抜き
	sen nuki
a broom	箒
	hooki
a can opener	缶切り
	kankiri
cleaning supplies	クリーニング用品
	kuriiningu yoohin
a corkscrew	コルクスクリュー
	koruku sukuryuu
detergent	洗剤
	senzai
dishwashing liquid	中性洗剤
	tyuusee senzai
garbage [rubbish] bags	ごみ袋
	gomi bukuro

a light bulb	電球
	denkyuu
matches	マッチ
	matchi
a mop	モップ
	moppu
napkins	ナプキン
	napukin
paper towels	ペーパータオル
	peepaa taoru
plastic wrap [cling film]	ラップ
	rappu
a plunger	トイレの吸引具
	toire no kyuuingu
scissors	はさみ
	hasami
a vacuum cleaner	掃除機
	soojiki

For In the Kitchen, see page 185.

AT THE HOSTEL

Do you have any places left for tonight?	今晩、空いている部屋はありますか。
	konban aiteiru heya wa arimasuka
Can I have...?	…をお願いします。
	...o onegai shimasu
a single/ double room	一人/二人部屋
	hitori/futari beya
a blanket	毛布
	moofu
a pillow	枕
	makura

sheets	**シーツ**
	shiitsu
a towel	**タオル**
	taoru
Do you have lockers?	**ロッカーはありますか。**
	rokkaa wa arimasu ka
What time do you lock up?	**正面玄関は、何時に閉まりますか。**
	shoomen genkan wa nanji ni shimarimasu ka
Do I need a membership card?	**メンバーシップカードは必要です か。**
	menbaa shippu kaado wa hitsuyoo desu ka
Here's my international student card.	**こちらが国際学生証です。**
	kochira ga kokusai gakusei shoo desu

There are over 500 youth hostels, or **ユースホステル** **yuusu hosuteru**, located in every part of Japan. They offer the most inexpensive accommodations available. You will often need to share rooms or bathrooms.

GOING CAMPING

Can I camp here?	**ここでキャンプできますか。**
	koko de kyanpu dekimasu ka
Is there a campsite near here?	**この近くに、キャンプ場はありますか。**
	kono chikaku ni kyanpujoo wa arimasu ka
What is the charge per day/week?	**一日/一週間の料金はいくらですか。**
	ichi-nichi/isshuukan no ryookin wa ikura desu ka

Are there...?	…はありますか 。
	...wa arimasu ka
cooking facilities	炊事場
	suijiba
electrical outlets	電源
	dengen
laundry facilities	洗濯場
	sentakuba
showers	シャワー
	shawaa
tents for hire	貸しテント
	kashi tento
Where can I empty the chemical toilet?	ケミカルトイレの汚物を処理したいんです が。
	kemikaru toire no obutsu o shori shitain desu ga

For Domestic Items, see page 80.

YOU MAY SEE...

飲料水	drinking water
キャンプ禁止	no camping
焚火/バーベキュー禁止	no fires/ barbecues

COMMUNICATIONS

NEED TO KNOW

Where's an internet café?	インターネットカフェはどこですか。 *intaanetto kafe wa doko desu ka*
Can I access the internet/check e-mail?	インターネット/Eメールを使いたいんです が。 *intaanetto/iimeeru o tsukaitain desu ga*
How much per (half) hour?	一(半)時間いくらですか。 *ichi(han)jikan ikura desu ka*
How do I connect / log on?	接続/ログオンしたいんですが。 *setsuzoku/roguon shitain desu ga*
I'd like a phone card, please.	テレホンカードをください。 *terehon kaado o kudasai*
Can I have your phone number?	電話番号を教えてください。 *denwa bangoo o oshiete kudasai*
Here's my number/ e-mail address.	これが私の電話番号/Eメールアドレ スです。 *kore ga watashi no denwabangoo/ iimeeru adoresu desu*
Call me.	電話してください。 *denwa shite kudasai*
E-mail me.	メールをください。 *meeru o kudasai*
Hello. This is…	もしもし。…ですが。 *moshi moshi…desu ga*
I'd like to speak to…	…さん、お願いします。 *…san onegai shimasu*
Could you repeat that, please?	もう一度、言ってください。 *moo ichido itte kudasai*

I'll call back later.	あとで電話します。
	ato de denwa shimasu
Bye.	ごめんください。
	gomen kudasai
Where's the post office?	郵便局はどこですか。
	yuubinkyoku wa doko desu ka
I'd like to send this to…	これを…に送りたいんですが。
	kore o…ni okuri tain desu ga

ONLINE

Where's an internet cafe?	インターネットカフェはどこですか。
	intaanetto kafe wa doko desu ka
Does it have wireless internet?	ワイアレスインターネットがありますか。
	waiaresu intaanetto ga arimasu ka
How do I turn the computer on/off?	コンピュータを点け/消したいんですが。
	konpyuuta o tsuke/keshi tain desu ga
What is the WiFi password?	無線LANのパスワードは何ですか。
	musen LAN no pasuwaado wa nandesuka
Is the WiFi free?	無線LAN は無料ですか 。
	musen LAN wa muryoo desuka

Can I access Skype?	スカイプにアクセスできますか
	sukaipu ni akusesu deki masu ka
Do you have bluetooth?	**Bluetooth はありますか**
	bluu twuusu wa ari masu ka
Can I...?	…いいですか。
	...iidesuka
plug in/charge my laptop/iPhone/iPad?	ラップトップ /iPhone/iPad の電源をつないでも/を充電しても
	rapputoppu/ai fon/ai paddo no dengen o tsunaidemo/o juuden shitemo
Can I...?	…がができますか。
	...ga dekimasu ka
access the internet	インターネットアクセス
	intaanetto akusesu
check e-mail	E メールのチェック
	iimeeru no chekku
print	印刷
	insatsu
How much per (half) hour?	一(半)時間いくらですか。
	ichi(han)jikan ikura desu ka
How do I...?	…はどうしますか。
	...wa doo shimasu ka
connect	接続する
	setsuzoku suru
disconnect	接続を切るの
	setsuzoku o kiru no
log on/off	ログオン/ログオフするの
	roguon/roguofu suru no
type this symbol	この記号をタイプするの
	kono kigoo o taipu suru no
What's your e-mail?	E メールのアドレスは何ですか。
	iimeeru no adoresuwa nan desu ka

My e-mail is...	私のEメールアドレスは…
	watashi no iimeeru adoresu wa...
Do you have a scanner?	スキャナーはありますか。
	sukyanaa wa arimasu ka

SOCIAL MEDIA

Are you on Facebook/Twitter?	Facebook/Twitter に参加していますか。
	feisu bukku/tsuittaa ni sanka shite imasu ka
What's your user name?	ユーザーネームは何ですか。
	yuuzaa neemu wa nan desu ka
I'll add you as a friend.	友達に追加します。
	tomodachi ni tsuika shimasu
I'll follow you on Twitter.	Twitter でフォローします。
	tsuittaa de foroo shimasu
Are you following...?	…をフォローしていますか。
	...o foroo shite imasu ka
I'll put the pictures on Facebook/Twitter.	Facebook/Twitter に写真を載せます。
	feisu bukku / tsuittaa ni shashin o nose masu
I'll tag you in the pictures.	あなたの写真にタグをつけます。
	anatano shashin ni tagu o tsuke masu

YOU MAY SEE...

閉じる	close
削除する	delete
Eメール	e-mail
ログアウト	exit
ヘルプ	help
インスタント・メッセージ	instant messenger
インターネット	internet
ログイン	login
新着メール	new (message)
オン/オフ	on/off
開ける	open
印刷する	print
保存	save
送信	send
ユーザー名/パスワード	username/ password
無線インターネット/ ワイヤレスインター ネット	wireless internet

PHONE

A phonecard/ prepaid phone, please.	テレホンカード/プリペイド携帯をお願いします。 *terehonkaado/puripeidokeitai o onegai shimasu*
How much?	いくらですか。 *ikura desuka*
What's the area/ country code for...?	…の市外局番/国番号は何番ですか。 *...no shigaikyokuban/kunibangoo wa nanban desu ka*

What's the number for Information?	番号案内は何番ですか。
	bangoo an-nai wa nanban desu ka
I'd like the number for…	…の番号を教えてください。
	…no bangooo oshiete kudasai
Where's the pay phone?	公衆電話はどこですか。
	koosyuu denwa wa doko desu ka
My phone doesn't work here.	私の電話が使えません。
	watashi no denwa ga tsukaemasen
What network are you on?	どの電話会社をご使用ですか。
	dono denwa gaisha o goshiyoo desu ka
Is it 3G?	3Gですか。
	3G desu ka
I have run out of credit/minutes.	クレジット/分数を使い果たしてしまいました。
	kurejitto/funsuu o tsukai hatashite shimai mashita
Can I buy some credit?	クレジットを買いたいのですが。
	kurejitto o kaitai no desu ga
A prepaid phone, please.	プリペイドフォンをお願いします。
	puripeido fon o onegai shimasu
Do you have a phone charger?	携帯用の充電器はありますか。
	keitaiyoo no juudenki wa arimasu ka
Can I have your number?	電話番号を教えてください。
	denwa bangoo o oshiete kudasai
Here's my number.	これが私の電話番号です。
	korega watashi no denwa bangoo desu
Call me.	電話してください。
	denwa shite kudasai
Text me.	携帯にメールを送ってください。
	keitai ni meeru o okutte kudasai
I'll call you.	電話します。
	denwa shimasu
I'll text you.	メールを送ります。
	meeru o okurimasu

YOU MAY HEAR...

どなたですか。 *donata desu ka*	Who's calling?
少々お待ちください。 *shoo shoo omachi kudasai*	Hold on.
おつなぎします。 *otsunagi shimasu*	I'll put you through.
すみません。今、出ています。 *sumimasen ima dete imasu*	I'm afraid he's/she's not in.
ただ今、電話に出られません。 *tada ima denwa ni deraremasen*	He/She can't come to the phone.
ご伝言を承りましょうか。 *godengon o uketamawarimashoo ka*	Would you like to leave a message?
後程/十分後にお電話ください。 *nochihodo/juppungoni odenwa kudasai*	Call back later/in 10 minutes.
こちらからお電話いたしましょうか。 *kochira kara odenwa itashimashoo ka*	Can he/she call you back?
お電話番号を頂けますか。 *odenwa bangoo o itadakemasu ka*	What's your number?

You can find public phones in hotel lobbies, on the street and in train stations. You will be able to make overseas phone calls using coins, prepaid telephone cards purchased at a convenience store, or your credit card. Country codes: Canada and US are +1, UK is +44. Directory assistance in English: 0120-364-463 110 (police) or 119 (fire).

TELEPHONE ETIQUETTE

Hello. This is…	もしもし。…ですが。
	moshi moshi…desu ga
I'd like to speak to…	…さん、お願いします。
	…san onegai shimasu
Extension…	内線…番
	naisen…ban
Speak louder/more slowly, please.	もう少し大きい声で/ゆっくりお願いします。
	mooo sukoshi ookii koe de/yukkuri onegai shimasu
Could you repeat that, please?	もう一度、言ってください。
	moo ichido itte kudasai
I'll call back later.	あとで電話します。
	atode denwa shimasu
Bye.	ごめんください。
	gomen kudasai

FAX

Can I send/receive a fax here?	ここでファックスを送れ/受け取れますか。
	kokode fakkusu o okure/uketore masu ka
What's the fax number?	ファックスの番号を頂けますか。
	fakkusu no bangoo o itadakemasu ka
Please fax this to…	これを…にファックスしてください。
	kore o…ni fakkusu shite kudasai

POST

Where's the post office/mailbox [postbox]?	郵便局/郵便ポストはどこですか。
	yuubinkyoku/yuubin posuto wa doko desu ka

Main post offices are open from 8:00 a.m. to 7:00 p.m. on weekdays, 9:00 a.m. to 5:00 p.m. on Saturdays and 9:00 a.m. to 12:30 p.m. on Sundays. Local post offices do not open on Sundays and will have limited hours mid-week. Tokyo International Post Office is open around the clock. Stamps are also sold at hotels and some tobacconists. Mailboxes, usually red, are found on street corners. You can also mail letters at hotels.

A stamp for this postcard/letter, please.	この葉書/手紙用の切手をください。 *kono hagaki/tegami yoo no kitte o kudasai*
How much?	いくらですか 。 *ikura desuka*
I want to send this package by airmail/express	この小包を速達/航空便で送りたいんですが。 *kono kozutsumi o sokutatsu/kookuubin de okuritain desu ga*
A receipt, please.	レシートをお願いします。 *reshiito o onegai shimasu*

YOU MAY HEAR...

税関申告書に記入してください。 *zeikan shinkokusho ni kinyuu shite kudasai*	Please fill out the customs declaration form.
どのくらいの値段のものですか。 *dono kurai no nedan no mono desu ka*	What's the value?
中には何が入っていますか。 *naka niwa nani ga haitte imasu ka*	What's inside?

SIGHTSEEING

NEED TO KNOW

Where's the tourist information office?	観光案内所はどこですか。
	kankoo annaijo wa doko desu ka
What are the main points of interest?	観光名所はどこですか。
	kankoo meesho wa doko desu ka
Do you have tours in English?	英語のツアーがありますか。
	eego no tsuaa ga arimasu ka
Could I have a map/guide please?	地図/案内書をください。
	chizu/annaisho o kudasai

TOURIST INFORMATION

Can you recommend...?	…はありますか。
	...wa arimasu ka
a boat trip	遊覧船
	yuuransen
an excursion	遊覧旅行
	yuuran ryokoo
a sightseeing tour	観光ツアー
	kankoo tsuaa
Do you have any information on...?	…の案内はありますか。
	...no annai wa arimasu ka

ON TOUR

I'd like to go on the tour to...	…へのツアーに参加したいんですが。
	...e no tsuaa ni sanka shitain desu ga
When's the next tour?	英語のツアーがありますか。
	sugi no tsuaa wa itsu desu ka

🛈

The Japan National Tourist Organization (JNTO) operates Tourist Information Centers (TIC) in Japan and overseas.These centers provide a wealth of information, including free maps, brochures, tour itineraries and advice on travel to and within Japan. They will give advice on the 'goodwill guide', a free service, as well as professional guide services.

In Tokyo, at Tokyo and Shinjuku rail stations,you will find special centers called Information for Foreigners (**gaikokujin annai jo**) providing foreigners with information on sightseeing, travel, living in Tokyo and much more.

Are there tours in English?	英語のツアーがありますか。 *eego no tsuaa ga arimasu ka*
Is there an English-speaking guide/ audio guide?	英語のガイド/オーディオがありますか。 *eego no gaido/oodio ga arimasu ka*
What time do we leave/return?	何時に出ますか/ 戻りますか。 *nanji ni demasu ka/modorimasu ka*
We'd like to have a look at the…	…を見たいんですが。 *…o mitain desu ga*
Can we stop here…?	…ここで止まれますか。 *…koko de tomaremasu ka*
to take photographs	写真を撮りたいんですが、 *shashin o toritain desu ga*
to buy souvenirs	お土産を買いたいんですが、 *omiyage o kaitain desu ga*
to use the bathrooms [toilets]	トイレに行きたいんですが、 *toire ni ikitain desu ga*
Is there access for the disabled?	身体障害者は入れますか。 *shintai shogaisha wa hairemasu ka*

For Tickets, see page 47.

SEEING THE SIGHTS

Where is the...?	**…はどこですか。**
	...wa doko desu ka
art gallery	**美術館**
	bijutsukan
battle site	**戦場跡**
	senjoo ato
botanical garden	**植物園**
	shokubutsuen
Buddhist temple	**お寺**
	otera
castle	**お城**
	oshiro
castle remains	**城跡**
	shiro ato
cemetery	**墓地**
	bochi
church	**教会**
	kyookai
downtown area	**繁華街**
	hankagai
fountain	**噴水**
	funsui
historic site	**史跡**
	shiseki
(war) memorial	**(戦争)記念碑**
	(sensoo) kinen hi
museum	**博物館**
	hakubutsukan
five-story [storey]	**五重塔**
pagoda	*gojuu no too*
Imperial palace	**皇居**
	kookyo

Where is the...?	**...はどこですか。**
	...wa doko desu ka
park	**公園**
	kooen
parliament	**国会議事堂**
building	*kokkai gijidoo*
Shinto shrine	**神社**
	jinja
shopping area	**商店街**
	shootengai
statue	**銅像**
	doozoo
theater [theatre]	**劇場**
	gekijoo
town hall	**市役所**
	shiyakusho
Can you show me on	**この地図で教えてください。**
the map?	*kono chizu de oshiete kudasai*
It's...	**...ですね。**
	...desu ne
amazing	**すごい**
	sugoi
beautiful	**美しい**
	utsukushii
boring	**つまらない**
	tsumaranai
interesting	**おもしろい**
	omoshiroi
magnificent	**立派**
	rippa
romantic	**ロマンチック**
	romanchikku
strange	**変**
	hen

superb	素晴らしい	
	subarashii	
terrible	ひどい	
	hidoi	
ugly	醜い	
	minikui	
I like it./I don't like it.	好きです/好きではありません。	
	suki desu/dewa arimasen	

For Asking Directions, see page 65.

RELIGIOUS SITES

Where's…?	…はどこですか。	
	…wa doko desu ka	
the cathedral	大聖堂	
	daiseedoo	
the Catholic/	カトリック/プロテスタント教会	
Protestant church	*katorikku/purotesutanto kyookai*	
the mosque	回教寺院	
	kaikyoo jiin	
the Shinto shrine	神社	
	jinja	
the synagogue	ユダヤ教会堂	
	yudaya kyookaidoo	
the Buddhist/	寺/禅寺	
Zen temple	*tera/zendera*	
What time is mass/	ミサ / 礼拝 は何時ですか。	
the service?	*misa/reehai wa nanji desu ka*	

LEISURE TIME

SHOPPING

NEED TO KNOW

Where is the shopping center?	ショッピングセンターはどこですか。
	shoppinngu sentaa wa doko desu ka
I'm just looking.	ちょっと見ているだけです。
	chotto miteiru dake desu
Can you help me?	ちょっと, お願いします。
	chotto onegai shimasu
I'm being helped.	大丈夫です。
	daijoobu desu
How much?	いくらですか。
	ikura desu ka
That one.	それ
	sore
That's all, thanks.	それで結構です。
	sorede kekkoo desu
Where can I pay?	どこで払うんですか。
	doko de haraun desu ka
I'll pay in cash/by credit card.	現金/(クレジット)カードで払います。
	genkin/(kurejitto) kaado de haraimasu
A receipt, please.	レシートをお願いします。
	reshiito o onegai shimasu

AT THE SHOPS

Where's the...?	…はどこですか。
	...wa doko desu ka
antiques store	骨董品店
	kottoohinten

Japanese people usually shop at department stores for clothing and household items. You will not be able to bargain at department stores, which tend to sell more expensive items. There are two large, upscale shopping centers, Roppongi Hills and Omote Sando Hills, in Tokyo. If you want to find bargain items, visit a flea market at the neighborhood temple or town square, where vendors sell used kimonos, household items or antiques. If you are interested in small electronic items such as audio-video equipment, home appliances, computers, computer games or anime and anime related characters, visit Akihabara in Tokyo. Several blocks surrounding the Akihabara Station are filled with stores selling all kinds of items.

bakery	パン屋
	pan ya
bank	銀行
	ginkoo
bookstore	本屋
	hon ya

clothing store	洋服屋
	yoofukuya
delicatessen	デリカテッセン
	derikatessen
department store	デパート
	depaato
health food store	健康食品店
	kenkoo shokuhin ten
jeweler	宝石店
	hooseki ten
liquor store	酒屋
	sakaya
[off-licence]	
market	マーケット
	maaketto
pastry shop	ケーキ屋
	keekiya
pharmacy	薬局
[chemist]	*yakkyoku*
produce [grocery]	食料品店
store	*shokuryoohin ten*
shoe store	靴屋
	kutsuya
shopping mall	ショッピングセンター
[shopping centre]	*shoppinngu sentaa*
the souvenir store	お土産屋
	omiyageya
the supermarket	スーパー
	suupaa
the tobacconist	タバコ屋
	tabakoya
the toy store	おもちゃ屋
	omochaya

For Souvenirs, see page 119.

YOU MAY HEAR...

いらっしゃいませ。	Welcome!
irasshaimase	
少々お待ちください。	One moment.
shooshoo omachi kudasai	
何がよろしいですか。	What would you like?
nani ga yoroshii desu ka	
他に何かございますか。	Anything else?
hoka ni nanika gozaimasu ka	

ASK AN ASSISTANT

What are the opening hours?	開店時間は何時ですか。
	kaiten jikan wa nanji desu ka
Where is/are...?	…はどこですか。
	…wa doko desu ka
the cashier [cash desk]	**会計**
	kaikee
the escalator	**エスカレーター**
	esukareetaa
the elevator [lift]	**エレベーター**
	erebeetaa
the fitting room	**試着室**
	shichakushitsu
the store directory [guide]	**店内の案内**
	tennai no annai
Can you help me?	**ちょっと、お願いします。**
	chotto onegai shimasu
I'm just looking.	**ちょっと見ているだけです。**
	chotto miteiru dake desu
I'm being helped.	**大丈夫です。**
	daijoobu desu

Do you have...?	...は、ありますか。
	...wa arimasu ka
Could you show me...?	...を見せてください。
	...o misete kudasai
Can you ship/wrap it?	届けて/包装してください。
	todokete/hoosoo shite kudasai
How much?	いくらですか。
	ikura desu ka
That's all, thanks.	それで全部です。
	sore de zenbu desu

For Clothing, see page 111.

YOU MAY SEE...

開店/閉店	open/closed
kaiten/heeten	
昼食のため休業中	closed for lunch
chuusyoku no tame kyuugyoo chuu	
試着室	fitting room
shichakushitsu	
お会計	cashier
okaikei	
現金のみ	cash only
genkin nomi	
クレジットカードも受け付けます	credit cards accepted
kurejitto kaado mo uketsuke masu	
営業時間	business hours
eigyoo jikan	
出口	exit
deguchi	

PERSONAL PREFERENCES

I'd like something…	…のが欲しいんですが。
	…no ga hoshiin desu ga
cheap/expensive	安い/高い
	yasui/takai
larger/smaller	もっと大きい/小さい
	motto ookii/chiisai
from this region	この地方から
	kono chihoo kara
Is it real?	本物ですか。
	honmono desu ka
Could you show me this/that?	これ/それを見せてください。
	kore/sore o misete kudasai
That's not quite what I want.	私が思っているのと少し違うんですが。
	watashi ga omotte iru noto sukoshi chigaun desu ga
No, I don't like it.	あまり好きではありません。
	amari suki dewa arimasen
That's too expensive.	高すぎます。
	taka sugimasu
I'd like to think about it.	考えさせてください。
	kangae sasete kudasai
I'll take it.	それにします。
	sore ni shimasu

PAYING & BARGAINING

How much?	いくらですか。
	ikura desu ka
I'll pay.	…で払います。
	…de haraimasu
in cash	現金
	genkin

YOU MAY HEAR...

お支払いはどうなさいますか。
oshiharai wa doo nasaimasu ka
このカードで承認が得られませんでした。
kono kaado de shoonin ga eraremasen deshita
他に身分証明はお持ちですか
hoka ni mibun shoomeisho wa omochi desu ka
現金でお願レ, します。
genkin de onegai shimasu
小銭はございますか。
kozeni wa gozaimasu ka

How are you paying?
This transaction has not been approved.
May I have additional identification?
Cash only, please.
Do you have any smaller change?

by credit card	**(クレジット)カード**
	(kurejitto) kaado
by traveler's check [cheque]	**トラベラーズチェック**
	toraberaazu chekku
A receipt, please.	**レシートをお願いします。**
	reshiito o onegai shimasu
That's too much.	**高すぎます。**
	taka sugimasu
I'll give you…	**…でどうですか。**
	…de doo desu ka
I only have…yen.	**…円しかありません。**
	…en shika arimasen
Is that your best price?	**もっと安くなりませんか。**
	motto yasuku narimasen ka
Can you give me a discount?	**割引してくれませんか。**
	waribiki shite kuremasen ka

Visitors to Japan can use the international credit cards at most stores, however, withdrawing cash using your credit card is limited to a small number of ATMs.

MAKING A COMPLAINT

I'd like...	…ですが 。
	...desu ga
to exchange this	**交換したいん**
	kookan shitain
to return this	**返品したいん**
	henpin shitain
a refund	**返金してもらいたいん**
	henkin shite moraitain
to see the manager	**マネージャーに会いたいん**
	maneejaa ni aitain

SERVICES

Can you recommend...?	いい…はありますか。
	ii...wa arimasu ka
a barber	**床屋**
	tokoya
a dry cleaner	**ドライクリーニング店**
	dorai kuriiningu ten
a hairdresser	**美容院**
	biyooin
a laundromat [launderette]	**コインランドリー**
	koin randorii
a nail salon	**ネイルサロン**
	neeru saron

a spa	スパ
	supa
a travel agency	旅行代理店
	ryokoo dairiten
Can you...this?	…できますか。
	...dekimasu ka
alter	仕立て直し
	shitatenaoshi
clean	洗濯
	sentaku
mend	修繕
	shuuzen
press	プレス
	puresu
When will it be ready?	いつできますか。
	itsu dekimasu ka

For Days, see page 26.

HAIR & BEAUTY

I'd like...	…をお願いしたいんですが。
	...o onegaishitain desu ga
an appointment for today/ tomorrow	今日/明日の予約
	kyoo/ashita no yoyaku
some color	カラー
	karaa
some highlights	ハイライト
	hairaito
my hair styled	スタイル
	sutairu
a haircut	カット
	katto

I'd like a trim.	そろえてもらいたいんですが。
	soroete moraitain desu ga
Don't cut it too short.	**切りすぎないでください。**
	kiri suginai de kudasai
Shorter here.	**ここをもう少し短くして下さい。**
	koko o moo sukoshi mijikaku shite kudasai
I'd like...	**...をお願いしたいんですが。**
	o onegai shitain desuga
an eyebrow/bikini wax	**眉毛/ビキニワックス**
	mayuge/bikini wakkusu
a facial	**フエーシヤノレ**
	feesharu
a manicure	**マニキュア**
	manikyua
pedicure	**ペディキュア**
	pedikyua
a (sports) massage	**(スポーツ)マッサージ**
	supootsu massaaji
Do you do...?	**...をしますか。**
	...o shimasu ka
acupuncture	**鍼**
	hari
aromatherapy	**アロマセラピー**
	aromaserapii

i

For relaxation in a traditional setting, visit one of many hot springs throughout Japan. You will find special facilities at hotels and Japanese inns near hot spring areas. A hot spring is enjoyed just like a bath: traditionally no bathing suit is worn, and there are separate areas for men and women. Sometimes you will find a smaller area for family use. In addition to the hot springs, there are many day spas in the cities, and hotel and resort spas are also available. Prices are comparable to the west, but tipping is not expected.

oxygen treatment	酸素治療 *sanso chiryoo*
Is there a sauna?	サウナがありますか。 *sauna ga arimasu ka*

For Pharmacy, see page 149.

ANTIQUES

How old is this?	どのくらい古いですか。 *dono kurai furui desu ka*
Do you have anything of the…era?	…時代のものはありますか。 *…jidai no mono wa arimasu ka*
Will I have problems with customs?	税関で問題になりますか。 *zeekan de mondai ni narimasu ka*
Is there a certificate of authenticity?	鑑定書はありますか。 *kanteesho wa arimasu ka*

For Souvenirs, see page 119.

CLOTHING

I'd like.	…が欲しいんですが。
	…ga hoshiin desu ga
Can I try this on?	**これを試着できますか。**
	kore o shichaku dekimasu ka
It doesn't fit.	**身体に合いません。**
	karada ni aimasen
It's too…	**…すぎます。**
	…sugimasu
big	**大き**
	ooki
small	**小さ**
	chiisa
short	**短**
	mijika
long	**長**
	naga
Do you have this in size…?	**これで…サイズのはありますか。**
	korede… saizu no wa arimasu ka
Do you have this in a bigger/smaller size?	**もう少し大きい/小さいのがありますか。**
	moo sukoshi ookii/chiisai no ga arimasu ka

For Numbers, see page 20.

YOU MAY SEE…

紳士服	men's clothing
婦人服	women's clothing
子供服	children's clothing

YOU MAY HEAR...

とてもよくお似合いです。
totemo yoku oniai desu
いかがですか。
ikaga desu ka
お客様に合うサイズがありません。
okyaku sama ni au saizu ga arima sen

That looks
great on you.
How does it fit?

We don't have
your size.

COLORS

I'm looking for something in...	…のを探しているんですが。 *…no o sagashite irun desu ga*
beige	ベージュ *beeju*
black	黒い *kuroi*
blue	ブルー *buruu*
brown	茶色 *chairo*
green	グリーン *guriin*
gray [grey]	グレー *guree*
orange	オレンジ色 *orenji iro*
pink	ピンク *pinku*
purple	紫 *murasaki*
red	赤い *akai*

white	**白い**
	shiroi
yellow	**黄色**
	kiiro

CLOTHES & ACCESSORIES

backpack	**リュックサック**
	ryukkusakku
belt	**ベルト**
	beruto
bikini	**ビキニ**
	bikini
blouse	**ブラウス**
	burausu
bra	**ブラジャー**
	burajaa
coat	**コート**
	kooto
dress	**ワンピース**
	wanpiisu
hat	**帽子**
	booshi
jacket	**上着**
	uwagi
jeans	**ジーパン**
	jiipan
pajamas	**パジャマ**
	pajama
panties	**パンティー (女性用の下着)**
(women's underwear)	*pantii (joseiyoo no shitagi)*
pants [trousers]	**ズボン**
	zubon

panty hose [tights]	パンスト
	pansuto
purse [handbag]	ハンドバッグ
	handobaggu
raincoat	レインコート
	einkooto
scarf	スカーフ
	sukaafu
shirt (men's)	ワイシャツ
	waishatsu
shorts	半ズボン
	hanzubon
skirt	スカート
	sukaato
socks	靴下
	kutsushita
suit	スーツ
	suutsu
sunglasses	サングラス
	sangurasu
sweater	セーター
	seetaa
sweatshirt	トレーナー
	toreenaa
swimsuit	水着
	mizugi
T-shirt	Tシャツ
	tii shatsu
tie	ネクタイ
	nekutai
underpants	ノベンツ
	pantsu

FABRIC

I'd like...	**...が欲しいんですが。**
	...ga hoshiin desu ga
cotton	**綿/コットン**
	men/kotton
denim	**デニム**
	denimu
lace	**レース**
	reesu
leather	**革**
	kawa
linen	**麻**
	asa
silk	**絹**
	kinu
wool	**ウール**
	uuru
Is it machine washable?	**洗濯機で洗えますか。**
	sentakuki de araemasu ka

SHOES

I'd like...	**…が欲しいんですが 。**
	...ga hoshiin desu ga
high-heeled/flat shoes.	**ハイヒール/平らな靴**
	haihiiru/taira na kutsu
boots	**ブーツ**
	buutsu
loafers	**ローファー**
	roofaa
sandals	**サンダル**
	sandaru

shoes	靴
	kutsu
slippers	スリッパ
	surippa
sneakers	スニーカー
	suniikaa
In size…	サイズ…の
	saizu…no

SIZES

small (S)	小
	shoo
medium (M)	中
	chuu
large (L)	大
	dai
extra large (XL)	特大
	tokudai
petite	プチサイズ
	puchi saizu
plus size	大きいサイズ
	ookii saizu

In Friendship stores and places where clothes are made for export, sizes will be given as small, medium and large. Most other clothing stores feature Chinese measurements that combine height and chest size; these measurements appear in centimeters. For example, if you are 170 cm tall (5'6") with a chest measurement of 90 cm (36"), look for clothing marked 170/90. Children's sizes are given by height, in centimeters.

NEWSAGENT & TOBACCONIST

Do you sell English-language books/newspapers?	英語の本/新聞はありますか。 *eego no hon/shinbun wa arimasu ka*
I'd like…	…が欲しいんですが。 *…ga hoshiin desu ga*
candy [sweets]	キャンデー *kyandee*
chewing gum	ガム *gamu*
a chocolate bar	チョコレート *chokoreeto*
cigars	葉巻 *hamaki*
a pack/carton of cigarettes	煙草一箱/一カートン *tabako hitohako/ichi kaaton*
a lighter	ライター *raitaa*
a magazine	雑誌 *zasshi*

matches	マッチ *matchi*
a newspaper	新聞 *shinbun*
a pen	ボールペン *boorupen*
a postcard	絵葉書 *ehagaki*
a road/town map of...	…の道路/市街地図 *...no dooro/shigai chizu*
stamps	切手 *kitte*

PHOTOGRAPHY

I'm looking for a(n)...camera.	…カメラを探しているんですが。 *...kamera o sagashite irun desu ga*
automatic	オートマチック *ootomachikku*
digital	デジタル *dejitaru*
disposable	使い捨て *tsukaisute*
I'd like...	…が欲しいんですが。 *...ga hoshiin desu ga*
a battery	電池 *denchi*
digital prints	デジタルカメラプリント *dejitaru kamera purinto*
a memory card	メモリーカード *memorii kaado*
Can I print digital photos here?	デジタル写真をプリントできますか。 *dejitaru shashin o purinto dekimasu ka*

SOUVENIRS

dolls	人形
	ningyoo
electrical goods	電気製品
	denki seehin
fans	扇子
	sensu
cloth wrap	風呂敷
traditionally used as	*furoshiki*
a handbag	
handcrafts	工芸品
	koogeehin
kimono	着物
	kimono
lacquerware	漆器
	shikki
ornaments	装飾品
	sooshokuhin
paper crafts	紙細工
	kami zaiku
pearls	真珠
	shinju
porcelain	磁器
	jiki
pottery	焼き物
	yakimono
prints	版画
	hanga
sake (rice wine)	日本酒
	nihonshu
woodblock prints	木版
	mokuhan

yukata (cotton bathrobe)	浴衣	
	yukata	
Can I see this/that?	これ/それをお願いします。	
	kore/sore o onegai shimasu	
It's the one in the window/display case.	ショーウインドー/ケースにあるのです。	
	shoouindoo/keesu ni aru no desu	
I'd like.	…が欲しいんですが。	
	…ga hoshiin desu ga	
a battery	電池	
	denchi	
a bracelet	ブレスレット	
	buresuretto	
a brooch	ブローチ	
	buroochi	
earrings	イヤリング	
	iyaringu	
a necklace	ネックレス	
	nekkuresu	
a ring	指輪/リング	
	yubiwa/ringu	
a watch	腕時計	
	ude dokee	
I'd like…	…が欲しいんですが。	
	…ga hoshiin desu ga	
copper	銅	
	doo	
crystal (quartz)	水晶	
	suishoo	
diamonds	ダイアモンド	
	daiamondo	
white/yellow gold	プラチナ/金	
	purachina/kin	

pearls	**真珠** *shinju*
pewter	**ピューター** *pyuutaa*
platinum	**プラチナ** *purachina*
sterling silver	**純銀** *jungin*
Is this real?	**本物ですか。** *honmono desu ka*
Can you engrave it?	**…を彫り込んでください。** *...o horikonde kudasai*

You will have no difficulty finding any number of souvenirs and presents to take home. There is something for everybody and in every price range. If you are buying electrical goods, remember that Japan uses 100 volts and that television/video systems may not be compatible. Different regions have their own specialties: you'll find pottery in Mashiko (north of Tokyo), **Bizen** (a specific type of pottery) in Okayama and lacquer-ware (called **shikki**) in Aizu (in Fukushima prefecture), Wajima (in Ishikawa prefecture) and Hida Takayama (in Gifu prefecture). You may also be interested in bamboo products, which are produced throughout Japan.

SPORT & LEISURE

NEED TO KNOW

When's the game?	試合はいつですか。
	shiai wa itsu desu ka
Where's…?	…はどこですか。
	…wa doko desu ka
the beach	ビーチ
	biichi
the park	公園
	kooen
the pool	プール
	puuru
Is it safe to swim/ dive here?	ここで泳いでも/飛び込んでも大丈夫 です。
	kokode oyoidemo/tobikondemo daijoobu desu ka
Can I rent [hire] golf clubs?	ゴルフクラブを借りたいんですが。
	gorufu kurabu o karitain desu ga
How much per hour?	料金は1時間いくらですか。
	ryookin wa ichijikan ikura desu ka
How much per round? (when hiring court)	1試合につきいくらですか。
	hitoshiai ni tsuki ikura desuka
How far is it to…?	…まで、どのくらいありますか。
	…made dono kurai arimasu ka
Can you show me on the map?	この地図で教えてください。
	kono chizu de oshiete kudasai

WATCHING SPORT

When's...?	…はいつですか。
	…wa itsu desu ka
the basketball game	バスケットボール
	basuketto booru no shiai
the baseball game	野球の試合
	yakyuu no shiai
the boxing match	ボクシングの試合
	bokushingu no shiai
the cycling race	自転車レース
	jitensha reesu
the golf tournament	ゴノレフトーナメント
	gorufu toonamento
the soccer game	サッカーの試合
	sakkaa no shiai
the tennis match	テニスの試合
	tenisu no shiai
the volleyball game	バレーボールの試合
	bareebooru no shiai
Which teams are playing?	どのチームが出ますか。
	dono chiimu ga demasu ka
Where's...?	…はどこですか。
	…wa doko desu ka

Most sports that are popular in the West — such as golf, tennis, football, basketball, etc. — are also popular in Japan. Many cities have martial arts halls in which you can watch **kendoo**, **juudoo**, **aikidoo** and **karate**. Japan's real national sport is **sumoo** (wrestling). This is an ancient, highly ritualized sport providing a true spectacle. There are six tournaments a year, each lasting 15 days. These are held in January, May, and September in Tokyo; in March in Osaka; July in Nagoya; November in Fukuoka. Skiing is also very popular in this mountainous country, and there are numerous ski resorts. It is best to reserve ski accommodations before you leave.

the horsetrack	競馬場	
	keebajoo	
the racetrack	競馬場	
	keebajoo	
the stadium	スタジアム	
	sutajiamu	
Where can I place a bet?	どこで賭け金を払いますか。	
	doko de kakekin o haraimasu ka	

PLAYING SPORT

Where's...?	…はどこですか。	
	...wa doko desu ka	
the golf course	ゴルフ場	
	gorufujoo	
the gym	スポーツジム	
	supootsu jimu	
the park	公園	
	kooen	

the tennis courts	テニスコート
	tenisu kooto
How much per...	**料金は**
	…いくらですか。
	ryookin wa …ikura desu ka
day	**日**
	nichi/hi
hour	**時間**
	jikan
game	**試合**
	shiai
round	**ラウンド**
	raundo
Can I rent [hire]...?	**…を借りられますか。**
	...o kariraremasu ka
golf clubs	**クラブ**
	kurabu
equipment	**道具**
	doogu
a racket	**ラケット**
	raketto

AT THE BEACH/POOL

Where's the beach/pool?	**ビーチ/プールはどこですか。**
	biichi/puuru wa doko desu ka
Is there...?	**…はありますか。**
	...wa arimasu ka
a kiddie pool	**子供用のプール**
	kodomo yoo no puuru
an indoor/outdoor pool	**屋内/屋外プール**
	okunai/okugai puuru
a lifeguard	**プール監視員**
	puuru kanshiin

Is it safe...?	**…大丈夫ですか。**
	…daijoobu desu ka
to swim	**泳いでも**
	oyoidemo
to dive	**飛び込んでも**
	tobikondemo
for children	**子供に**
	kodomo ni
I want to rent [hire]…	**…を借りたいんですが。**
	…o karitain desu ga
a deck chair	**デッキチェア**
	dekki chea
diving equipment	**スキューバダイビング用具**
	sukyuuba daibingu yoogu
a jet-ski	**ジェットスキー**
	jetto sukii
a motorboat	**モーターボート**
	mootaa booto
a rowboat	**ボート**
	booto
snorkeling equipment	**シュノーケル**
	shunookeru
a surfboard	**サーフボード**
	saafuboodo
a towel	**タオル**
	taoru

Beaches close to Tokyo and Osaka can be very
crowded in the summer, and until September 1, when
summer officially ends. Okinawa, the Amakusa Islands, the
Yaeyama Islands are good for snorkeling and scuba diving.

an umbrella	パラソル
	parasoru
water skis	水上スキー
	suijoo sukii
a windsurfer	ウインドサーフィン
	uindo saafin
For...hours.	…時間
	...jikan

WINTER SPORTS

A lift pass for a day/ five days, please.	一日/五日分のリフト券、お願いします。
	ichinichi/itsuka bun no rifutoken onegai shimasu
I want to rent [hire]...	…を借りたいんですが。
	...o karitain desu ga
boots	スキー靴
	sukii gutsu
a helmet	ヘルメット
	herumetto
poles	ストック
	sutokku
skis	スキー
	sukii

a snowboard	スノーボード *sunoo boodo*
snowshoes	スノーシューズ *sunooshuuzu*
These are too big/small.	大き/小さすぎます。 *ooki/chiisa sugimasu*
Are there lessons?	レッスンがありますか *ressun ga arimasu ka*
I'm a beginner.	初心者です。 *shoshinsha desu*
I'm experienced.	経験者です。 *keekensha desu*
A trail [piste] map, please.	ゲレンデマップ、お願いします。 *gerende mappu onegai shimasu*

YOU MAY SEE...

ケーブルカー	cable car
リフト	chair lift
初心者	novice
中級	intermediate
上級	expert
コーズ閉鎖中	trail [piste] closed

You will find opportunities for both downhill and cross-country skiing in Japan. Many travelers choose to combine skiing with the delights of a **ryokan** or **minshuku** (traditional Japanese guest houses) offering a hot spa.

OUT IN THE COUNTRY

I'd like a map of...	…の地図をください。
	…no chizu o kudasai
this region	**この地域**
	kono chiiki
the walking routes	**ハイキングコース**
	haikingu koosu
bike routes	**サイクリングコース**
	saikuringu koosu
the trails	**ハイキング**
	haikingu
Is it easy/difficult?	**やさしい/難しいですか。**
	yasashii/muzukashii desu ka
Is it far/steep?	**遠い/急斜面ですか。**
	tooi/kyuushamen desu ka
How far is it to...?	**…まで、どのくらいありますか。**
	…made dono kurai arimasu ka
Can you show me on the map?	**この地図で教えてください。**
	kono chizu de oshiete kudasai
I'm lost.	**道に迷いました。**
	michi ni mayoimashita
Where's the...?	**…はどこですか。**
	…wa doko desu ka

bridge	橋
	hashi
cave	洞窟
	dookutsu
canal	運河
	unga
cliff	崖
	gake
farmhouse	農家
	nooka
field	野原
	nohara
forest	森
	mori
hill	丘
	oka
island	島
	shima
lake	湖
	mizuumi
mountain	山
	yama
mountain pass	山道
	yama michi
mountain range	山脈
	sanmyaku
nature reserve	自然保護区域
	shizen hogo kuiki
panorama	展望
	tenboo
park	公園
	kooen
peak	山頂
	sanchoo

plain	**平野**
	heeya
pond	**池**
	ike
rapids	**急流**
	kyuuryuu
river	**川**
	kawa
hot spring	**温泉**
	onsen
stream	**小川**
	ogawa
valley	**谷間**
	tanima
viewpoint	**展望台**
	tenboo dai
village	**村**
	mura
waterfall	**滝**
	taki
wood	**林**
	hayashi

TRAVELING WITH CHILDREN

NEED TO KNOW

Is there a discount for children?	子供の割引はありますか。
	kodomo no waribiki wa arimasu ka
Can you recommend a baby sitter?	信頼できるベビーシッターを教えてください。
	shinrai dekiru bebii shittaa o oshiete kudasai
Could we have a child's seat/ highchair?	子供用の椅子/ハイチェアをお願いします。
	kodomo yoo no isu/hai chea o onegai shimasu
Where can I change the baby?	おむつはどこで替えられますか。
	omutsu wa doko de kaeraremasu ka

OUT & ABOUT

Can you recommend something for the kids?	子供が楽しめるところを教えてください。 *kodomo ga tanoshimeru tokoro o oshiete kudasai*
Where's...?	…はどこですか *...wa doko desu ka*
the amusement park	遊園地 *yuuenchi*
the arcade	ゲームセンター *geemu sentaa*
the kiddie [paddling] pool	子供用のプール *kodomo yoo no puuru*
the playground	公園 *kooen*
the zoo	動物園 *doobutsu en*
Are kids allowed?	子供でも入れますか。 *kodomo demo hairemasu ka*
Is it safe for kids?	子供でも大丈夫ですか。 *kodomo demo daijoobu desu ka*
Is it suitable for... year olds?	…歳の子供でも大丈夫ですか。 *...sai no kodomo demo daijoobu desu ka*

BABY ESSENTIALS

Do you have...?	…は、ありますか。 *...wa arimasu ka*
a baby bottle	哺乳瓶 *honyuubin*
baby wipes	お尻拭き *oshiri fuki*
a car seat	チャイルドシート *chairudo shiito*

a children's menu	お子さまメニュー
	okosama menyuu
a child's seat/	子供用のイス/ハイチェア
highchair	*kodomo yoo no isu/haichea*
a crib	ベビーベッド
	bebii beddo
diapers [nappies]	(紙)おむつ
	(kami) omutsu
formula	ミルク
	miruku
a pacifier [soother]	おしゃぶり
	oshaburi
a playpen	ベビーサークル
	bebii saakuru
a stroller	ベビーカー
[pushchair]	*bebiikaa*
Can I breastfeed the baby here?	ここで授乳してもいいですか。
	kokode junyuu shitemo ii desu ka
Where can I change the baby?	おむつはどこで替えられますか。
	omutsu wa doko de kaeraremasu ka

YOU MAY HEAR...

かわいい！	How cute!
kawaii	
お名前は？	What's his/her
onamae wa	name?
何歳ですか。	How old is he/
nansai desu ka	she?

BABYSITTING

Can you recommend a reliable baby sitter?	信頼できるベビーシッターを教えてください。
	shinrai dekiru bebii shittaa o oshiete kudasai
What's the charge?	料金 はいくらですか。
	ryookin wa ikura desu ka
I'll pick them up at...	…に迎えに 行きます。
	...ni mukae ni ikimasu
I can be reached at...	…に電話してください。
	...ni denwa shite Kudasai

For Time, see page 25.

SAFE TRAVEL

EMERGENCIES

NEED TO KNOW

Help!	**助けて!** *tasukete*
Go away!	**あっちへ行け!** *atchi e ike*
Call the police!	**警察を呼んで!** *keesatsu o yonde*
Stop thief!	**泥棒!** *doroboo*
Get a doctor!	**医者を呼んで!** *isha o yonde*
Fire!	**火事だ!** *kaji da*
I'm lost.	**道に迷いました。** *michi ni mayoimashita*
Can you help me?	**助けてください。** *tasukete kudasai*

In an emergency, dial: **110** for the police;
119 for the fire brigade and emergency medical
services.

YOU MAY HEAR...

この用紙に記入してください。
kono yooshi ni kinyuu shite kudasai

身分証明書を見せてください。
mibun shoomeisho o misete kudasai

いつ/どこで起きたんですか。
itsu/dokode okitan desu ka

どんな顔をしていますか。
donna kao o shite iamsu ka

Please fill out
this form.

Your
identification,
please.

When/Where
did it happen?

What does he/
she look like?

POLICE

NEED TO KNOW

Call the police!	警察を呼んで! *keesatsu o yonde*
Where's the police station?	交番はどこですか。 *kooban wa doko desu ka*
There has been an accident/attack.	事故がありました/襲われました。 *jiko ga arimashita/osowaremashita*
My child is missing.	子供がいなくなりました。 *kodomo ga inaku narimashita*
I need an interpreter.	通訳が要るんですが。 *tsuuyaku ga irun desu ga*
I need…	…したいんですが。 *…shitain desu ga*
to contact my lawyer	弁護士に連絡 *bengoshi ni renraku*
to make a phonecall	電話 *denwa*
I'm innocent.	無実です。 *mujitsu desu*

CRIME & LOST PROPERTY

I want to report…	…を報告したいんですが。 *…o hookoku shitaindesu ga*
a mugging	強盗 *gootoo*
a rape	レイプ *reepu*

a theft	泥棒 *doroboo*
I've been mugged.	強盗にあいました。 *gootoo ni aimashita*
I've lost my…	…をなくしました。 *…o nakushimashita*
My…has been stolen	…を盗まれました。 *…o nusumaremashita*
backpack	リュックサック *ryukkusakku*
bicycle	自転車 *jitensha*
camera	カメラ *kamera*
car	車 *kuruma*
rental car	レンタカー *renta kaa*
computer	コンピュータ *konpyuuta*
credit cards	クレジットカード *kurejitto kaado*
jewelry	宝石 *hooseki*
money	お金 *okane*
passport	パスポート *pasupooto*
purse/wallet	財布 *saifu*
traveler's checks [cheques]	トラベラーズチェック *toraberaazu chekku*

I need a police report for my insurance claim.	保険の申請に警察の証明書が要ります。 *hoken no shinsee ni keesatsu no shoomeesho ga irimasu*
Where is the British/American/Irish embassy?	英国/アメリカ/アイルランド大使館はどこですか。 *eikoku/amerika/airurando taishikan wa doko desu ka*
I need an interpreter.	通訳が必要です。 *tsuuyaku ga hitsuyoo desu*

HEALTH

NEED TO KNOW

I'm sick.	具合が悪いんです。 *guai ga waruin desu*
I need an English-speaking doctor.	英語ができる医者はいますか。 *eego ga dekiru isha wa imasu ka*
It hurts here.	ここが痛いんです。 *koko ga itain desu*
I have a stomachache.	お腹が痛いんです。 *onaka ga itain desu*

FINDING A DOCTOR

Can you recommend a doctor/dentist?	医者/歯医者を教えてください。 *isha/haisha o oshiete kudasai*
Could the doctor come to see me here?	往診してくれますか。 *ooshin shite kuremasu ka*

I need an English-speaking doctor.	英語ができる医者はいますか。
	eego ga dekiru isha wa imasu ka
What are the office hours?	診察時間はいつですか。
	shinsatsu jikan wa itsu desu ka
Can I make an appointment…?	…予約したいんですが。
	…yoyaku shitain desu ga
for today	今日
	kyoo
for tomorrow	明日
	ashita
as soon as possible	できるだけ早く
	dekirudake hayaku
It's urgent.	至急お願いします。
	shikyuu onegai shimasu

SYMPTOMS

I'm…	しています。
	shite imasu
bleeding	出血
	shukketsu
constipated	便秘
	benpi
dizzy	目眩
	memai
It hurts here.	ここが痛いんです。
	koko ga itai n desu
I'm nauseous/vomiting.	吐きそうです/吐いています。
	hakisoo desu/haite imasu
I have…	…があります。
	…ga arimasu
an allergic reaction	アレルギー反応
	arerugii hannoo

chest pain	胸の痛み
	mune no itami
an earache	耳の痛み
	mimi no itami
a fever	熱
	netsu
pain	痛み
	itami
a rash	発疹
	hasshin
some swelling	腫れ
	hare

YOU MAY HEAR...

どうしましたか。
doo shimashita ka
What's wrong?

どこが痛みますか。
doko ga itamimasu ka
Where does it hurt?

ここが痛みますか。
koko ga itamimasu ka
Does it hurt here?

他に薬を飲んでいますか。
hokani kusuri o nonde imasu ka
Are you taking any other medication?

何かのアレルギーはありますか。
nanka no arerugii wa arimasu ka
Are you allergic to anything?

口を開けてください。
kuchi o akete kudasai
Open your mouth.

深呼吸してください。
shin kokyuu shite kudasai
Breathe deeply.

病院に行ってください。
byooin ni itte kudasai
Please go to the hospital.

I have a sprain.	ねんざしました。
	nenza shimashita
I have a stomachache.	お腹が痛いんです。
	onaka ga itain desu
I have sunstroke.	日射病にかかりました。
	nisshabyoo ni kakarimashita
I've been sick for... days	…日間, 病気です。
	...nichikan byooki desu

CONDITIONS

I'm...	…です。
	...desu
anemic	貧血症
	hinketsu shoo
asthmatic	ぜんそく
	zensoku
diabetic	糖尿病
	toonyoo byoo
epileptic	てんかん症
	tenkanshoo

I'm allergic to antibiotics/penicillin.	抗生物質/ペニシリンにアレルギーがあります。
	koosei busshitsu/penishirin ni arerugii ga arimasu
I have arthritis.	関節炎にかかっています。
	kansetsuen ni kakatte imasu
I have (high/low) blood pressure.	高/低血圧です。
	koo/tei ketsuatsu desu
I have a heart condition.	心臓が悪いんです。
	shinzoo ga waruin desu
I'm on...	…を飲んでいます。
	...o nonde imasu
I'm ...months pregnant.	妊娠…ヶ月です。
	ninshin ... ka getsu desu

TREATMENT

Do I need a prescription/ medicine?	処方箋/薬が必要ですか。
	shohoo sen/kusuri ga hitsuyoo desu ka
Can you prescribe a generic drug [unbranded medication]?	後発医薬品を処方してもらえますか。
	koohatsu iyakuhin o shohoo shite morae masu ka

Where can I get it? **どこで買えますか。**
doko de kae masu ka

For What to Take, see page 150.

HOSPITAL

Please notify my family. **家族に知らせてください。**
kazoku ni shirasete kudasai

I'm in pain. **痛みます。**
itamimasu

I need a doctor/nurse. **医者/看護師を呼んでください。**
isha/kangoshi o yonde kudasai

When are visiting hours? **面会時間はいつですか。**
menkai jikan wa itsu desu ka

I'm visiting. **…の見舞いに来ました。**
…no mimai ni kimashita

DENTIST

I've broken a tooth/lost a filling. **歯を折りました/詰め物をなくしました。**
ha o orimashita/tsumemono o nakushimashita

I have a toothache. **歯が痛いんです。**
ha ga itain desu

Can you fix this denture? **この入れ歯を直せますか。**
kono ireba o naosemasu ka

GYNECOLOGIST

I have menstrual cramps/a vaginal infection. **生理痛/膣感染症があります。**
seeritsuu/chitsu kansen shoo ga arimasu

I missed my period.	生理がありませんでした。
	seeri ga arimasen deshita
I'm on the Pill.	ピルを飲んでいます。
	piru o nonde imasu
I'm pregnant/not pregnant.	妊娠しています/いません。
	ninshin shite imasu/imasen
I haven't had my period for…months.	生理が…ヶ月間ありません。
	seeri ga… kagetsukan arimasen

OPTICIAN

I've lost.	…をなくしました。
	…o nakushimashita
one of my contact lenses	片方のコンタクトレンズ
	katahoo no kontakuto renzu
my glasses	眼鏡
	megane
a lens	レンズ
	renzu

PAYMENT & INSURANCE

How much?	いくらですか。
	ikura desuka
Can I pay by credit card?	クレジットカードを使えますか。
	kurejitto kaado o tsukaemasu ka
I have insurance.	保険に入っています。
	hoken ni haitte imasu
Can I have a receipt for my insurance?	保険申請のためにレシートをください。
	hoken shinsee no tame ni reshiito o kudasai

PHARMACY

NEED TO KNOW

Where's the nearest (all-night) pharmacy?	（夜間営業の）薬局はどこですか。 *(yakan eegyoo no) yakkyoku wa doko desu ka*
What time does the pharmacy open/close?	薬局は何時に開き/閉まりますか。 *yakkyoku wa nanji ni aki/shimari masu ka*
What would you recommend for...?	…には何がいいですか。 *...niwa nani ga ii desu ka*
How much should I take?	どのくらい飲むんですか。 *dono kurai nomun desu ka*
Can you fill [makeup] this prescription for me?	この薬をください。 *kono kusuri o kudasai*
I'm allergic to...	私は…にアレルギーがあります。 *watashi wa... ni arerugii ga arimasu*

ℹ️

You will find a large selection of imported medications at the American Pharmacy in Tokyo. These can be more expensive than at home, so if you have any special medical needs it is best to bring an ample supply with you.

WHAT TO TAKE

How much should I take?	どのくらい飲むんですか。
	dono kurai nomun desu ka
How many times a day should I take it?	一日何回飲むんですか。
	ichinichi nankai nomun desu ka
Is it suitable for children?	子供でも飲めますか。
	kodomo demo nomemasu ka
I'm taking…	…を飲んでいます。
	…o nonde imasu
Are there side effects?	副作用はありますか。
	fukusayoo wa arimasu ka
I'd like some medicine for…	…の薬をください。
	…no kusuri o kudasai
a cold	風邪
	kaze
a cough	咳
	seki
diarrhea	下痢
	geri
a headache	頭痛
	zutsuu
a toothache	歯が痛い
	haga itai
I'd like some medicine for…	…の薬をください。
	…no kusuri o kudasai

insect bites	虫刺され
	mushi sasare
motion [travel] sickness	乗物酔い
	norimono yoi
a sore throat	喉の痛み
	nodo no itami
sunburn	日焼け
	hiyake
an upset stomach	胃痛
	itsuu

YOU MAY SEE...

一日一回／三回	once/three times a day
錠	tablet(s)
滴	drop
ティースプーン／茶さじ	teaspoon(s)
食前／食後／食間	before/after/in between meals
空腹時	on an empty stomach
丸ごと飲み下し	swallow whole
眠気を催すことがあります	may cause drowsniness
外用薬	for external use only

BASIC SUPPLIES

I'd like...

…が欲しいんですが 。

…ga hoshiin desu ga

acetaminophen [paracetamol]	アセタミノーフェン *asetaminoofen*
antiseptic cream	傷薬 *kizugusuri*
aspirin	頭痛薬 *zutsuuyaku*
bandages	包帯 *hootai*
a comb	櫛 *kushi*
condoms	コンドーム *kondoomu*
contact lens solution	コンタクトレンズ液 *kontakutorenzu eki*
deodorant	デオドラント *deodoranto*
a hairbrush	ヘアブラシ *heaburashi*
hair spray	ヘアスプレー *hea supuree*
ibuprofen	イブプロフェン *ibupuroren*
insect repellent	防虫剤 *boochuuzai*
a nail file	ネイルファイル *neirufairu*
a (disposable) razor	(使い捨て) カミソリ *(tsukaisuite) kamisori*
razor blades	カミソリの刃 *kamisori no ha*

sanitary napkins [pads]	生理用ナプキン	*seeri yoo napukin*
shampoo/ conditioner	シャンプー/コンディショナー	*shanpuu/kondishonaa*
soap	石鹸	*sekken*
sunscreen	日焼け止めクリーム	*hiyake dome kuriimu*
tampons	タンポン	*tanpon*
tissues	ティッシュペーパー	*tisshu peepaa*
toilet paper	トイレットペーパー	*toiretto peepaa*
toothpaste	歯磨き粉	*hamigakiko*

For Baby Essentials, see page 133.

CHILD HEALTH & EMERGENCY

Can you recommend a pediatrician?	小児科医を教えてください。 *shoonikai o oshiete kudasai*
My child is allergic to…	うちの子供は…にアレルギーがあります。 *uchi no kodomo wa…ni arerugii ga arimasu*
My child is missing.	子供がいなくなりました。 *kodomo ga inaku narimashita*
Have you seen a boy/girl?	男/女の子を見ましたか。 *otoko/onna no ko o mimashita ka*

For Police, see page 140.

DISABLED TRAVELERS

NEED TO KNOW

Is there…?	…はありますか。
	…wa arimasu ka
access for the disabled	身体障害者用通路
	shintai shogaisha yoo tsuuro
a wheelchair ramp	車椅子用スロープ
	kuruma isu yoo suroopu
a handicapped [disabled] accessible toilet	ハンディキャップ用トイレ
	handikyappu yoo toire
I need…	… が要るんですが。
	…ga irun desu ga
assistance	助け
	tasuke
an elevator [lift]	エレベーター
	erebeetaa
a ground floor room	1 階の部屋
	ikkai no heya

Many provincial main stations have elevators and other facilities for disabled travelers. However, smaller stations generally do not.

ASKING FOR ASSISTANCE

I'm disabled.	私は身体が不自由です。
	watashi wa karada ga fujiyuu desu
I'm deaf.	私は耳が聞こえません。
	watashi wa mimi ga kikoemasen
I'm visually/hearing impaired.	私は目がよく見えません/耳がよく聞こえません。
	watashi wa me ga yoku miemasen/mimi ga yoku kikoemasen
I'm unable to walk far/use the stairs.	私は遠くまで歩けません/階段を上れません。
	watashi wa tooku made arukemasen/ kaidan o noboremasen
Can I bring my wheelchair?	車椅子を持っていってもいいですか。
	kurumaisu o motte ittemo ii desu ka
Are guide dogs permitted?	盲導犬が入ってもいいですか。
	moodooken ga haittemo ii desu ka
Can you help me?	助けてください。
	tasukete kudasai
Please open/hold the door.	ドアを開けて/開けておいてください。
	doa o akete/akete oite kudasai

FOOD

EATING OUT

NEED TO KNOW

Can you recommend a good restaurant/bar?	いいレストラン/バー をご存知ですか。 *ii resutoran/baa o gozonji desu ka*
Is there a traditional Japanese/inexpensive restaurant nearby?	この近くに料亭/安いレストランはあります か。 *kono chikaku ni ryootei/yasui resutoran wa arimasu ka*
A table for one/two, please.	一人/二人ですが、テーブルがあります か。 *hitori/futari desu ga, teeburu ga arimasu ka*
Could we sit...?	…に座れますか。 *...ni suwaremasu ka*
here/there	ここ/そこ *koko/soko*
outside	外 *soto*

in a non-smoking area	禁煙席 *kin en seki*
I'm waiting for someone.	人を待っているんです。 *hito o matte irun desu*
Where's the restroom [toilet]?	トイレはどこですか。 *toire wa doko desu ka*
A menu, please.	メニューをお願いします。 *menyuu o onegai shimasu*
What do you recommend?	何がおいしいですか。 *nani ga oishii desu ka*
I'd like…	…が欲しいんですが *…ga hoshiin desu ga*
Some more…, please.	…をお願いします。 *…o onegai shimasu*
Enjoy your meal.	どうぞごゆっくり。 *doozo goyukkuri*
The check [bill], please.	お勘定、お願いします。 *okanjoo onegai shimasu*
Is service included?	サービス料込みですか。 *saabisuryoo komi desu ka*
Can I pay by credit card?	クレジットカードを使えますか。 *kurejitto kaado o tsukaemasu ka*
Could I have a receipt, please?	レシートをお願いします。 *reshiito o onegai shimasu*
Thank you for the food.	ごちそうさまでした。 *gochisoo sama deshita*

WHERE TO EAT

Can you recommend…?	…はありますか。 *…wa arimasu ka*

a restaurant	レストラン
	resutoran
a bar	バー
	baa
a café	カフェ
	kafe
a fast-food place	ファストフードの店
	fasuto fuudo no mise
a sushi restaurant	寿司屋
	sushi ya
a cheap restaurant	安いレストラン
	yasui resutoran
an expensive restaurant	高いレストラン
	takai resutoran
a restaurant with a good view	眺めの良いレストラン
	nagame no yoi resutoran
an authentic/ a non-touristy restaurant	庶民的な/観光客向けでないレストラン
	syominteki na/kankookyaku muke de nai resutoran

RESERVATIONS & PREFERENCES

I'd like to reserve a table…	…予約をお願いしたいんですが。
	yoyaku o onegai shitai n desu ga
for 2	2人で
	futari de
for this evening	今晩
	konban
for tomorrow at…	明日…時に
	ashita…ji ni
Can I get a table in the shade/sun?	日陰の/日向のテーブルをお願いします。
	hikage no/hinata no teeburu o onegai shimasu

YOU MAY HEAR...

ご予約はいただいておりますでしょうか。 | Do you have a
goyoyaku wa itadaite orimasu deshoo ka | reservation?
何人様でしょうか。 | How many?
nannin sama deshoo ka |
喫煙席と禁煙席のどちらがよろしいですか。 | Smoking or
kitsuenseki to kin-enseki no dochira ga non-smoking?
yoroshii desu ka |
ご注文はお決まりですか。 | Are you ready
gochuumon wa okimari desu ka | to order?
何がよろしいですか。 | What would
nani ga yoroshii desu ka | you like?
…がお薦めです。 | I recommend…
…ga osusume desu |
どうぞごゆっくり。 | Enjoy your
doozo goyukkuri | meal.

A table for 2.	**2人、お願いします。**
	futari onegai shimasu
We have a	**予約してあります。**
reservation.	*yoyaku shite arimasu*
My name is…	**…です。**
	…desu
Could we sit…?	**…に座れますか。**
	…ni suwaremasu ka
here/there	**ここ/そこ**
	koko/soko
outside	**外**
	soto
in a non-smoking	**禁煙席**
area	*kin enseki*

by the window	窓際
	madogiwa
in the shade	日陰に
	hikage ni
in the sun	日向に
	hinata ni
Where are the restrooms [toilets]?	トイレはどこですか。 *toire wa doko desu ka*

HOW TO ORDER

Waiter!/Waitress!	ちょっとすみません。
	chotto sumimasen
We're ready to order.	注文したいんですが。
	chuumon shitain desu ga
May I see the wine list, please?	ワインリストをお願いします。 *wain risuto o onegai shimasu*
I'd like…	…が欲しいんですが 。
	…ga hoshiin desu ga
a bottle of…	…を一 本
	…o ippon
a carafe of…	…を一カラフ
	…o hito karafu
a glass of…	…一杯
	…ippai
The menu, please.	メニューをお願いします。
	menyuu o onegaishimasu
Do you have…?	…は、ありますか。
	…wa arimasu ka
a menu in English	英語のメニュー
	eigo no menyuu
a fixed price menu	セットメニュー
	setto menyuu

YOU MAY SEE...

カバーチャージ	cover charge
セット値段	fixed-price
メニュー	menu
本日のメニュー	menu of the day
サービス料金込(別)	service (not) included
スペシャル	specials

a children's menu	子供用のメニュー
	kodomo yoo no menyuu
What do you recommend?	何がおいしいですか。
	nani ga oishii desu ka
What's this?	これは何ですか。
	kore wan nan desu ka
What's in it?	何が入っていますか。
	nani ga haitte imasu ka
Is it spicy?	これは辛いですか。
	kore wa karai desu ka
Some more ..., please	…を、もう少しお願いします。
	...o moo sukoshi onegai shimasu
It's to go [take away].	持ち帰りです。
	mochi kaeri desu
With/Without...	…と/…無しで
	...to/...nashi de
I can't have...	…は食べられません。
	...wa taberaremasen
I'd like...	…が欲しいんですが。
	...ga hoshiin desu ga
More... please	…をもっとください。
	...o motto kudasai

For Drinks, see page 186.

COOKING METHODS

baked	**焼き**	*yaki*
boiled	**茹で**	*yude*
braised	**蒸し煮**	*mushini*
breaded	**パン粉**	*panko*
creamed	**クリームソース**	*kuriimu soosu*
diced	**さいの目切りの**	*sai no me giri no*
filleted	**切り身の**	*kiri mi no*
fried	**揚げ**	*age*
grilled	**焼き**	*yaki*
poached	**ポシェ**	*poshe*
roasted	**ロースト**	*roosuto*
sautéed	**炒めた**	*itameta*
smoked	**薫製**	*kunsei*
steamed	**蒸し**	*mushi*
stewed	**煮込み**	*nikomi*
stuffed	**詰め物**	*tsumemono*

DIETARY REQUIREMENTS

I am...	私は…です。
	watashi wa... desu
diabetic	糖尿病
	toonyoobyoo
lactose intolerant	乳糖不対症
	nyuutoo futaishoo
vegetarian	ベジタリアン
	bejitarian
vegan	ヴィーガン
	biigan
I'm allergic to...	…にアレルギーがあります。
	...ni arerugii ga arimasu
I can't eat...	…は食べられません。
	...wa taberaremasen
dairy	乳製品
	nyuuseehin
gluten	グルテン
	guruten
nuts	ナッツ
	nattsu
pork	豚肉
	buta niku
shellfish	貝類
	kairui
spicy foods	辛い食べ物
	karai tabemono
wheat	小麦
	komugi
Is it halal/kosher?	これはハラール/コーシャですか。
	kore wa haraaru/koosha desu ka
Do you have...?	…はありますか。
	...wa arimasu ka

skimmed milk	無脂肪乳
	mushiboo nyuu
whole milk	普通の牛乳
	futsuu no gyuunyuu
soya milk	豆乳
	toonyuu
I'm lactose intolerant…	私は乳製品アレルギーがあります。
	watashi ha nyuseihin arerugi ga arimasu.

DINING WITH CHILDREN

Do you have children's portions?	お子さまメニューはありますか 。
	okosama menyuu wa arimasu ka
A highchair, please.	子供のための椅子はありますか。
	kodomo no tame no isu wa arimasu ka
Where can I feed/ change the baby?	どこで授乳したら/おしめを取り替えたらいいでしょうか。
	doko de junyuu shitara/oshime o torikaetara ii deshoo ka
Can you warm this?	これを暖めてください。
	kore o atatamete kudaasai

HOW TO COMPLAIN

How much longer will our food be?	後、どのくらいかかりますか。
	ato dono kurai kakarimasu ka
We can't wait any longer.	もう待てません。
	moo matemasen
We're leaving.	帰ります。
	kaerimasu
I didn't order this.	注文したのと違います。
	chuumon shitano to chigaimasu
I ordered…	…を注文しました。
	…o chuumon shimashita

I can't eat this.	これは、食べられません。
	kore wa taberaremasen
This is too…	…すぎます。
	…sugimasu
cold/hot	冷た/熱
	tsumeta/atsu
salty/spicy	塩辛/辛
	shio kara/kara
tough/bland	固/味が薄
	kata/aji ga usu
This isn't clean/ fresh.	きれい/新鮮じゃありません。
	kiree/shinsen ja arimasen

PAYING

The check [bill], please.	お勘定、お願いします。
	okanjoo onegai shimasu
We'd like to pay separately.	別々に、お願いします。
	betsubetsu ni onegai shimasu
It's all together.	一緒にお願いします。
	issho ni onegai shimasu
Is service included?	サービス料込みですか。
	saabisu ryoo komi desu ka
What's this amount for?	これは何の金額ですか。
	kore wa nan no kingaku desu ka
I didn't have that.	それは取りませんでした。
	sore wa torimasen deshita.
I had…	注文したのは…です。
	chuumon shita nowa…desu
Can I pay by credit card?	クレジットカードを使えますか。
	kurejitto kaado o tsukaemasu ka
Can I have an itemized bill/ a receipt?	明細書/レシートをお願いします。
	meesaisho/reshiito o onegai shimasu

That was a very good meal.	おいしかった。ごちそうさまでした。 *oishikatta. gochisoo sama deshita*
I've already paid.	もう支払いは済ませました。 *moo shiharai wa sumase mashita*

Tipping is not a Japanese custom, and there is no need to tip at most restaurants, bars and **izakaya** (taverns). However, some places, especially high-end ones, may include a 'service charge' on the bill as gratuity.

MEALS & COOKING

In large Western-style hotels you will have your choice of breakfast: Japanese, English/American or Continental. However, in **ryokan** and **minshuku** (traditional Japanese lodgings) you will be offered only a Japanese-style breakfast. This usually consists of grilled, smoked fish (e.g. salmon), rice, soup and pickles served with tea. While you are out and about, coffee shops provide various dishes for breakfast, including thick slices of buttered toast.

BREAKFAST

ベーコン *beekon*	bacon
パン *pan*	bread

バター	butter
bataa	
(コールド/ホット)シリアル	(cold/hot) cereal
(koorudo/hotto) shiriaru	
チーズ	cheese
chiizu	
コーヒー/紅茶	coffee/tea
koohii/koocha	
砂糖入りの	with sugar
satoo iri no	
ダイエットシュガー 入りの	with artificial
daietto shugaa iri no	sweetner
ミルク入りの	with milk
miruku iri no	
カフェイン抜きの	decaf
kafein nuki no	
ブラック	black
burakku	
コールドカット	cold cuts
koorudo katto	[charcuterie]
卵	eggs
tamago	
ゆで卵	a boiled egg
yude tamago	
目玉焼き/スクランブルエッグ	fried/scrambled
medama yaki/sukuranburu eggu	eggs
フルーツジュース	fruit juice
furuutsu juusu	
アップル	apple
appuru	
グレープフルーツ	grapefruit
gureepufuruutsu	
オレンジ	orange
orenji	

グラノーラ *guranoora*	granola [muesli]
蜂蜜 *hachimitsu*	honey
ジャム *jamu*	jam
ミルク *miruku*	milk
マフィン *mafin*	muffin
オートミール *ooto miiru*	oatmeal
オムレツ *omuretsu*	omelet
ロールパン *rooru pan*	rolls
ソーセージ *sooseeji*	sausages
トースト *toosuto*	toast
水 *mizu*	water
ヨーグルト *yooguruto*	yogurt

APPETIZERS

オードブルの盛り合わせ *oodoburu no moriawase*	assorted appetizers
ハム *hamu*	ham
…が欲しいんですが 。 *…ga hoshiin desu ga*	I'd like…

…をもっとください。	More… please
…o motto kudasai	
おつまみ	Japanese snacks
otsumami	
漬物	Japanese pickled
tsukemono	vegetables
オリーブ	olives
oriibu	
牡蛎	oysters
kaki	
サラダ	salad
sarada	
サラミ	salami
sarami	

Otsumami are snacks that accompany drinks. You will find such things as salted rice crackers, nuts and dried cuttle fish.

SOUP

コンソメスープ	clear soup
konsome suupu	
ポタージュスープ	creamed soup
potaaju suupu	
すまし汁(お吸物)	Japanese clear
sumashi jiru (osuimono)	soup
みそ汁	miso soup
misoshiru	
コーンスープ	sweetcorn soup
koon suupu	

There are two kinds of Japanese soup, which is always part of a traditional meal: **misoshiru**, a light soup often with a few finely chopped piecaes of vegetable and bean curd, the distinctive flavor of which comes from the fermented bean paste (**miso**); and **sumashi jiru** or **suimono**, a clear soup, again with vegetables or bean curd.

In a Japanese meal the soup is not served as a first course, but together with the main course, or with boiled rice and other items.

野菜スープ *yasai suupu*	vegetable soup
寄せ鍋 *yosenabe*	thick soup of chicken, shellfish, prawns, bean curd and vegetables
ラーメン *raamen*	Chinese noodle broth with meat, fish, veg
吸物/すまし汁 *suimono/sumashi jiru*	clear soup of fish bouillon or seaweed
あんかけうどん *ankake udon*	wheat noodles in a thick bouillon with fish cake and vegetables
タンメン *tanmen*	Chinese noodle soup with fried veg
冷麦 *hiyamugi*	thinly cut wheat noodles and cold soup

ざるそば *zaru soba*	buckwheat noodles served with cold soup
冷やし中華 *hiyashi chuuka*	Chinese noodles sweet and sour sauce, sliced ham, fish cake and cucumber
おでん *oden*	a winter soup with veg, fish cake, eggs

FISH & SEAFOOD

鰹(カツオ) *katsuo*	bonito (mackerel family)
鱈(タラ) *tara*	cod
たらこ *tarako*	cod roe
ロブスター *robusutaa*	lobster
鯖(サバ) *saba*	mackerel
ムール貝 *muuru gai*	mussels
蛸(タコ) *tako*	octopus
牡蠣(カキ) *kaki*	oysters
鮭(サケ) *sake*	salmon
いくら *ikura*	salmon roe
帆立貝 *hotate gai*	scallop

Fish and seafood play a major role in Japanese cuisine. This is reflected in the variety and quality of available seafood. Typical ways of eating fish include broiled, boiled, deep fried and raw. Prepared raw fish (**sushi** or **sashimi**) is dipped into a mixture of soy sauce and **wasabi** (horseradish paste), and enjoyed with steaming hot rice. **Sashimi** is usually served as part of a larger meal, and **sashimi** restaurants are often expensive. You can also buy **sushi** at the food court of a department store, at a supermarket, or at a take-out restaurant.

いか *ika*	squid
海老(エビ) *ebi*	shrimp [prawns]
鱒(マス) *masu*	trout
鮪(マグロ) *maguro*	tuna
白子(シラス) *shirasu*	whitebait
刺身 *sashimi*	raw fish with soy and wasabi
寿司 *sushi*	rice balls with raw fish
焼き魚 *yaki zakana*	grilled fish
天ぷら *tenpura*	fresh fish, seafood and veg, deep-fried
天ぷらうどん *tenpura udon*	battered fish and veg in a noodle broth

煮魚 *ni zakana*	fish cooked in assorted sauces
ちり鍋 *chirinabe*	fish and veg broth

MEAT & POULTRY

ベーコン *beekon*	bacon
牛肉 *gyuu niku*	beef
鶏肉/チキン *tori niku/chikin*	chicken
鴨 *kamo*	duck
ひれステーキ *hire suteeki*	filet steak
ハム *hamu*	ham
ラム肉 *ramu niku*	lamb
レバー *rebaa*	liver
豚肉 *buta niku*	pork
ソーセージ *sooseeji*	sausages
ステーキ *suteeki*	steak
サーロインステーキ *saaroin suteeki*	sirloin steak
薄切り *usugiri*	thin slices

すき焼 *sukiyaki*	thin slices of beef, veg, bean curd, noodles
しゃぶしゃぶ *shabu shabu*	thinly sliced beef with veg in broth
焼肉 *yaki niku*	Grilled Korean marinated meat, veg
とんかつ *tonkatsu*	fried breaded pork cutlet with cabbage and rice
カツ丼 *katsudon*	deep fried pork with rice, egg, onion,peas
焼き鳥 *yakitori*	barbequed chicken in sweet soy sauce
レア *rea*	rare
ミディアム *midiamu*	medium
ウェルダン *werudan*	well-done

VEGETABLES & STAPLES

おひたし *ohitashi*	boiled green vegetables with soy sauce
豆 *mame*	beans
パン *pan*	bread
そば *soba*	buckwheat noodles

In a Japanese meal, rice is served separately in an individual bowl. It is short grained and slightly sticky. Although plain, rice is perhaps the most important part of the meal. The Japanese consider it a heresy to mix other food items or sauces into the rice. It is customary to raise the bowl to your lips and push the rice into your mouth with chopsticks. On a Western-style menu rice is usually called **raisu**. For egg and rice dishes, see On the Menu on page 195 under 'egg'.

キャベツ *kyabetsu*	cabbage
にんじん *ninjin*	carrot
白菜 *hakusai*	Chinese cabbage
ラーメン *raamen*	Chinese noodles in soup
きゅうり *kyuuri*	cucumber
なす *nasu*	eggplant [aubergine]
ぎんなん *ginnan*	gingko nut
さやいんげん *saya ingen*	green bean
漬物 *tsukemono*	Japanese pickled vegetables
ねぎ *negi*	leek
レタス *retasu*	lettuce

Salad isn't part of traditional Japanese cuisine; pickled vegetables are a more authentic equivalent. However, many Western-style restaurants and bars offer a variety of salads and dressings.

パスタ *pasuta*	pasta
味の素 *aji no moto*	MSG (monosodium glutamate)
マッシュルーム *masshuruumu*	mushroom
椎茸(しいたけ) *shiitake*	shitake mushroom
えのきだけ *enokidake*	enokidake mushroom
玉ねぎ *tamanegi*	onion
グリンピース *gurinpiisu*	pea
ポテト *poteto*	potato (in Western dishes)
じゃがいも *jagaimo*	potato (in Japanese dishes)
かぼちゃ *kabocha*	pumpkin
ご飯 *gohan*	rice
スパゲッティ *supagetti*	spaghetti
野菜炒め *yasai itame*	stir-fried vegetables

野菜の煮物	stewed vegetables
yasai no nimono	
トマト	tomato
tomato	
大根	white radish
daikon	
うどん	wheat noodles
udon	

Noodle dishes are very popular, and make delicious and filling meals. It's not considered bad manners to make slurping noises while eating your noodles — the extra oxygen is supposed to improve the taste. For dishes, see 'noodle' on page 200 in the On the Menu section.

FRUIT

りんご	apple
ringo	
バナナ	banana
banana	
さくらんぼ	cherry
sakuranbo	
グレープフルーツ	grapefruit
gureepufuruutsu	
ぶどう	grape
budoo	
メロン	melon
meron	
オレンジ	orange
orenji	

桃
momo

peach

梨
nashi

pear

柿
kaki

persimmon

苺(いちご)
ichigo

strawberry

蜜柑(みかん)
mikan

tangerine

西瓜(すいか)
suika

watermelon

DESSERT

餅
mochi

rice cake, traditionally eaten at New Year

あんみつ
anmitsu

gelatin cubes made from seaweed, with sweet bean paste and fruit

氷あずき
koori azuki

sweet bean paste covered with shaved ice and sweet syrup

フルーツみつ豆
furuutsu mitsumame

gelatin cubes made from seaweed, topped with fruit and syrup

プリン
purin

crème caramel

アイスクリーム
aisu kuriimu

ice cream

Dessert is not a typical part of a Japanese meal. Called **dezaato**, it was introduced from the West. Today you will find a variety of Western-style desserts along with a number of desserts made from more typical Japanese ingredients.

あんまん *anman*	hot steamed bun with sweet azuki bean paste
チョコレートパフェ *chokoreeto pafe*	chocolate parfait
葛餅 *kuzu moch*	arrowroot cake with molasses syrup
ホットケーキ *hotto keeki*	sweet pancake with butter and syrup
フルーツサラダ *furuutsu sarada*	fruit salad
おはぎ *ohagi*	balls of rice covered with bean paste
お汁粉 *oshiruko*	sweet red bean paste soup

SAUCES & CONDIMENTS

コショウ/胡椒 *koshoo*	black pepper
ケチャップ *kechappu*	ketchup
味噌 *miso*	miso (paste of fermented soybeans)
マスタード *masutaado*	mustard

塩	salt
shio	
醤油	soy sauce
shooyu	

> In Japan, goods are usually sold in small portions to
> avoid selling them in certain numbers as some numbers are
> considered bad luck. Vegetables are usually sold per piece,
> or in pre-packaged bags that are quite uniform in volume.
> The weight is not marked (e.g. a bag of potatoes contains
> five potatoes). Prices for fish vary according to type and
> season and are sold per unit, not by the kilogram.

AT THE MARKET

Where are the carts [trolleys]/baskets?	カート/かごはどこですか。
	kaato/kago wa doko desu ka
Where is…?	…はどこですか。
	…wa doko desu ka
I'd like some of that/ those.	それを少しください。
	sore o sukoshi kudasai
Can I taste it?	味見してもいいですか。
	ajimi shitemo ii desu ka
I'd like a kilo/ half-kilo of …	…が一キロ/五百グラム欲しいんですが
	…ga ichikiro/gohyakuguramu hoshiin desu ga
I'd like…	…が欲しいんですが
	…ga hoshiin desu ga
a liter/half-liter of…	…が一リットル/500cc
	… ga iti rittoru/gohyaku shiishii
a piece of	…が一個
	…ga ikko

a slice of	…が一枚
	…ga ichimai
More/Less than that	もう少し多く/少なく
	moo sukoshi ooku/sukunaku
How much?	いくらですか。
	ikura desuka
Where do I pay?	どこで払うんですか。
	doko de haraun desu ka
A bag, please.	袋をお願いします。
	fukuro o onegai shimasu
I'm being helped.	大丈夫です。
	daijoobu desu

YOU MAY SEE...

賞味期限…	best if used by…
カロリー	calories
無脂肪	fat free
要冷蔵	keep refrigerated
…を極少量含む	may contain traces of…
販売期限	sell by…
菜食主義者向け	suitable for vegetarians

IN THE KITCHEN

YOU MAY HEAR…

いらっしゃいませ。
irasshaimase

何がよろしいですか。
naniga yoroshii desu ka

他に何かございますか。
hokani nanika gozaimasu ka

…円でございます。
…en de gozaimasu

Can I help you?

What would
you like?
Anything else?

That's…yen.

For daily shopping, people usually go to a
neighborhood fish market, vegetable store, butcher or
grocer. Larger supermarkets are also popular, as well as food
floors of department stores (usually located in the basement)
where you'll find groceries and prepared food. In Tokyo there
is a famous fish market called **Tsukiji Uoichiba**, which is
open early in the morning. In Kyoto, **Nishiki Shijo** (Nishiki
Market) is called the kitchen of Kyoto. Here you can find all
kinds of local ingredients at more than one hundred stores.

bottle opener	栓抜き
	sennuki
bowl	ボール
	booru
can opener	缶切り
	kankiri
corkscrew	コルクスクリュー
	koruku sukuryuu
cups	カップ
	kappu
forks	フォーク
	fooku
frying pan	フライパン
	furaipan
glasses	グラス/コップ
	gurasu/koppu
knife	ナイフ
	naifu
measuring cup/ spoon	計量カップ/スプーン
	keeryoo kappu/supuun
napkin	ナプキン
	napukin
plates	皿
	sara
pot	深鍋
	fuka nabe
saucepan	鍋
	nabe
spatula	へら
	hera
spoon	スプーン
	supuun

DRINKS

NEED TO KNOW

May I see the wine list/drink menu?	ワインリスト/ドリンクメニュー を見せてください。
	wain risuto/dorinku menyuu o misete kudasai
What do you recommend?	何がおいしいですか。
	nani ga oishii desu ka
I'd like a bottle/glass of red/white wine.	赤/白ワインを一本/一杯お願いします。
	aka/shiro wain o ippon/ippai onegai shimasu
The house wine, please.	ハウスワインをお願いします。
	hausu wain o onegai shimasu
Another bottle/glass, please.	もう一本/一杯お願いします。
	moo ippon/ippai onegai shimasu
I'd like a local beer.	地ビールをお願いします。
	jibiiru o onegai shimasu
Can I buy you a drink?	一杯おごらせてください。
	ippai ogorasete kudasai
Cheers!	乾杯!
	kanpai
A coffee/tea, please.	コーヒー/紅茶をお願いします。
	koohii/koocha o onegai shimasu
Black	ブラック
	burakku
With…	…と
	…to
milk	ミルク
	miruku
sugar	砂糖
	satoo

artificial sweetener	ダイエットシュガー
	daietto shugaa
With/Without…	…と/…無しで
	…to/…nashi de
I can't have…	…は食べられません
	…wa taberaremasen
I'd like…	…をお願いします。
	…o onegai shimasu
juice	フルーツジュース
	furuutsu juusu
soda	炭酸飲料
	tansan inryoo
sparkling/still water	ソーダ水/水
	soda sui/mizu
Is the tap water safe to drink?	水道水は飲んでも安全ですか。
	suidoosui wa nondemo anzen desu ka

NON-ALCOHOLIC DRINKS

コーヒー	coffee
koohii	
ブラック	black
burakku	
ミルク入りの	with milk
miruku irino	
砂糖入りの	with sugar
satoo iri no	
ダイエットシュガー入りの	with artificial
daietto shugaa iri no	sweetner
アイスコーヒー	iced coffee
aisu koohii	

Sake is the general name for any drink, traditional or imported, but is usually used to refer to rice wine, more properly known as **nihonshu**.

Japanese green tea is often served in restaurants free of charge. It is drunk without any additions.

A special tea, **matcha** is used for traditional ceremonies. It was first used by Buddhist monks to help them stay awake while meditating. Its spiritual roots are still apparent today in the highly ritualized tea ceremony. The tea should not only refresh you physically, but also give you time to appreciate the beauty of the objects used in the ceremony and the surroundings, all leading to meditative reflection. You may find tea ceremony rooms in museums and gardens, where you'll be able to try a little **matcha** for a small fee.

Japanese	English
ココア *kokoa*	hot chocolate
ジュース *juusu*	juice
アップルジュース *appuru juusu*	apple juice
オレンジジュース *orenji juusu*	orange juice
レモネード *remoneedo*	lemonade
ミルク *miruku*	milk (when ordering at a restaurant)
ミルクセーキ *mirukuseeki*	milkshake
紅茶 *koocha*	tea

お茶
ocha

green tea

アイスティー
aisu tii

iced tea

水
mizu

water

ミネラルウォーター
mineraru wootaa

mineral water

ソーダ
sooda

soda water

トニック
tonikku

tonic water

YOU MAY HEAR...

何か飲みますか。
nani ka nomimasu ka

Can I get you a drink?

ミルク/砂糖を入れますか。
miruku/satoo o iremasu ka

With milk/ sugar?

炭酸水ですか,非炭酸水ですか。
tansansui desu ka hi tansansui desu ka

Sparkling or still water?

APERITIFS, COCKTAILS & LIQUEURS

シングル/ダブル
shinguru/daburu

single/double

ストレート/オンザロック
sutoreeto/onzarokku

straight [neat]/ on the rocks

グラス1杯/瓶1本
gurasu ippai/bin ippon

a glass/a bottle

ブランデー
burandee

brandy

ジン *jin*	gin
ジントニック *jin tonikku*	gin and tonic
梅酒 *umeshu*	plum wine
ラム酒 *ramu shu*	rum
シェリー/ベルモット *sherii/berumotto*	sherry/vermouth
焼酎 *shoochuu*	shoochuu
ウォッカ *wokka*	vodka
ウイスキー *uisukii*	whisky
水割り *mizuwari*	with water
ウイスキーソーダ *uisukii sooda*	with soda water

BEER

瓶入り *bin iri*	bottled
生 *nama*	draft [draught]
黒ビール *kuro biiru*	dark beer

WINE

赤ワイン *aka wain*	red wine

The Japanese produce a number of different beers which are similar to English and German lager beers. Three well known-brands are Asahi®, Kirin® and Sapporo®. In most bars you can choose between bottled and draft. **Shoochuu** is a distilled liquor (up to 90 proof) made from either sweet potatoes or rice. This drink is not commonly known to visitors to Japan and is held in rather low esteem by some Japanese. The best **shoochuu** is, however, excellent and is comparable to tequila, vodka, and other such spirits. Whisky is now a very popular drink in Japan and there are a number of good Japanese brands — the best known is probably Suntory®.

Grape wine isn't an authentic Japanese drink and until recently was not produced in Japan. You will not find wine widely available outside of Western-style restaurants, big hotels, and department stores. Even there you may find the choice limited to sweeter white wines, although this is changing.

Rice wine, known as **nihonshu** but usually referred to as **sake**, is the traditional Japanese wine. The snacks traditionally served with sake are known as **otsumami**. These include seafood and meat served on skewers, sweet-salty dried cuttlefish, sashimi and more.

This drink is served at table in small china carafes and is drunk from small cups or wooden boxes. You can ask for your **nihonshu** to be served cold, warm or hot.

白ワイン
shiro wain
white wine

ロゼ
roze
blush [rosé] wine

ドライ/スイート/スパークリング
dorai/suiito/supaakuringu
dry/sweet/sparkling

冷えた/室温の
hieta/shitsuon no
chilled/at room temperature

お酒/日本酒
osake/nihonshu
sake/nihonshu

  冷
  hiya
cold

  人肌
  hitohada
lukewarm

  熱燗
  atsukan
hot

ON THE MENU

アーモンド
aamondo
almond

食前酒
shokuzenshu
aperitif

りんご
ringo
apple

アップルジュース
appuru juusu
apple juice

アンズ
anzu
apricot

アーティチョーク
aatichooku
artichoke

ダイエットシュガー
daietto shugaa
artificial sweetner

アスパラバス　　　　　　　　asparagus
asuparagasu
アボカド　　　　　　　　　　avocado
abokado
ベーコン　　　　　　　　　　bacon
beekon
バナナ　　　　　　　　　　　banana
banana
バス　　　　　　　　　　　　bass
basu
ベイリーフ　　　　　　　　　bay leaf
bei riifu
豆　　　　　　　　　　　　　bean
mame
もやし　　　　　　　　　　　bean sprout
moyashi
牛肉　　　　　　　　　　　　beef
gyuu niku
ビール　　　　　　　　　　　beer
biiru
ビート　　　　　　　　　　　beet
biito
胡椒　　　　　　　　　　　　black pepper
koshoo
ロゼ　　　　　　　　　　　　blush [rosé] wine
roze
鰹(カツオ)　　　　　　　　　bonito (mackerel
katsuo　　　　　　　　　　family)
ブランデー　　　　　　　　　brandy
burandee
パン　　　　　　　　　　　　bread
pan
胸肉　　　　　　　　　　　　breast chicken
muneniku

コンソメ broth
konsome
そば buckwheat noodles
soba
バター butter
bataa
キャベツ cabbage
kyabetsu
にんじん carrot
ninjin
カリフラワー cauliflower
karifurawaa
セロリ celery
serori
チーズ cheese
chiizu
さくらんぼ cherry
sakuranbo
鶏肉 chicken
tori niku
ひよこ豆 chickpea
hiyoko mame
白菜 Chinese cabbage
hakusai
餃子 Chinese meat
gyooza dumplings
ラーメン Chinese noodle
raamen soup
チョコレート chocolate
chokoreeto
鱈(タラ) cod
tara
たらこ cod roe
tarako

コーヒー *koohii*	coffee
クッキー *kukkii*	cookie [biscuit]
コーンミール *koon miiru*	cornmeal
蟹 *kani*	crab
クラッカー *kurakkaa*	cracker
生クリーム *namakuriimu*	cream
きゅうり *kyuuri*	cucumber
カレー *karee*	curried
カスタード *kasutaado*	custard
揚げ *age*	deep-fried
するめ *surume*	dried squid
鴨 *kamo*	duck
餃子 *gyooza*	dumpling
鰻 *unagi*	eel
卵 *tamago*	egg
卵焼き *tamago yaki*	thick sweet omelet
目玉焼き *medama yaki*	fried eggs

オムレツ *omuretsu*	omelet
オムライス *omuraisu*	omelet with fried fried rice and ketchup
茶碗蒸し *chawan mushi*	egg custard with veg, fish and chicken
定食 *teeshoku*	set menu: rice, soup, fish or meat, pickles
炒飯 *chaahan*	fried rice with pork, egg, peas and shrimp
カレーライス *karee raisu*	Japanese curry
なす *nasu*	eggplant [aubergine]
エンダイブ *endaibu*	endive
キクヂシャ *kikujisha*	escarole
いちじく *ichijiku*	fig
魚 *sakana*	fish
蒲鉾 *kamaboko*	fish cake
ポテトフライ *poteto furai*	French fries [chips]
フルーツ/果物 *furuutsu/kudamono*	fruit
フルーツサラダ *furuutsu sarada*	fruit salad

ニンニク *ninniku*	garlic
ジン *jin*	gin
生姜 *shooga*	ginger
ぎんなん *ginnan*	gingko nuts
グラノーラ *guranoora*	granola [muesli]
グレープフルーツ *gureepufuruutsu*	grapefruit
ぶどう/葡萄 *budoo*	grape
さやいんげん *saya ingen*	green bean
お茶 *ocha*	green tea
焼き豆腐 *yaki doofu*	grilled tofu
グアバ *guaba*	guava
ハム *hamu*	ham
ハンバーガー *hanbaagaa*	hamburger
ヘーゼルナッツ *heezeru nattsu*	hazlenut
心臓 *shinzoo*	heart
ハーブ *haabu*	herb
ニシン *nishin*	herring

蜂蜜(ハニー) honey
hachimitsu (hanii)
ココア hot chocolate
kokoa
ホットドッグ hot dog
hotto doggu
氷 ice (cube)
koori
アイスクリーム ice cream
aisu kuriimu
アイスコーヒー iced coffee
aisu koohii
アイスティー iced tea
aisu tii
ジャム jam
jamu
漬物 Japanese pickled
tsukemono vegetables
おつまみ Japanese snacks
otsumami
カレーライス Japanese-style
karee raisu curry on rice
ジュース juice
juusu
ケチャップ ketchup
kechappu
キウィ kiwi
kiui
ラム肉 lamb
ramu niku
ねぎ/葱 leek
negi

もも肉 *momo niku*	leg
レモン *remon*	lemon
レモネード *remoneedo*	lemonade
平豆 *hiramame*	lentil
レタス *retasu*	lettuce
ライム *raimu*	lime
レバー *rebaa*	liver
ロブスター *robusutaa*	lobster
鯖(サバ) *saba*	mackerel
マンゴー *mangoo*	mango
マーガリン *maagarin*	margerine
マヨネーズ *mayoneezu*	mayonnaise
肉 *niku*	meat
メロン *meron*	melon
牛乳 *gyuunyuu*	milk (a carton)
ミルク *miruku*	milk (when ordering in a restaurant)
ミルクセーキ *mirukuseeki*	milkshake

ミネラルウォーター *mineraru wootaa*	mineral water
ミント *minto*	mint
味噌 *miso*	miso (paste made from fermented soybeans)
みそ汁 *misoshiru*	miso soup
味の素 *aji no moto*	MSG (monosodium glutamate)
マッシュルーム *masshuruumu*	mushrooms
ムール貝 *muuru gai*	mussels
からし *karashi*	mustard
マトン *maton*	mutton
うどん *udon*	noodle
そば *soba*	buckwheat noodle broth, meat or egg, veg
うどん *udon*	wheat-flour noodle broth, meat or egg,veg
ラーメン *raamen*	Chinese noodle broth
そうめん *soomen*	wheat-flour noodles
ヌガー *nugaa*	nougat

ナッツ	nuts
nattsu	
オートミール	oatmeal
ootomiiru	
蛸(タコ)	octopus
tako	
オリーブ	olive
oriibu	
オリーブオイル	olive oil
oriibu oiru	
オムレツ	omelet
omuretsu	
玉ねぎ	onion
tamanegi	
オレンジ	orange
orenji	
オレンジジュース	orange juice
orenji juusu	
オレガノ	oregano
oregano	
オックス	ox
okkusu	
オックステール	oxtail
okkusu teeru	
牡蛎	oyster
kaki	
パンケーキ	pancake
pankeeki	
パパイヤ	papaya
papaiya	
パプリカ	paprika
papurika	
パスタ	pasta
pasuta	

ペストリー
pesutorii
pastry

桃
momo
peach

ピーナッツ
piinattsu
peanut

梨
nashi
pear (Japanese pears)

グリンピース
gurinpiisu
pea

ピーカン
piikan
pecan

ピーマン
pepper
pepper (vegetable)

柿
kaki
persimmon

ピクルス
pikurusu
pickle [gherkin]

パイナップル
painappuru
pineapple

ピザ
piza
pizza

プラム
puramu
plum

豚肉
buta niku
pork

馬鈴薯/じゃがいも
bareesho/jagaimo
potato (Japanese dishes)

ポテト
poteto
potato (Western dishes)

ポテトチップ
poteto chippu
potato chips [crisps]

プルーン
puruun
prune

Japanese	Romaji	English
プリン	*purin*	pudding
かぼちゃ	*kabocha*	pumpkin
ウズラ	*uzura*	quail
ウサギ肉	*usagi niku*	rabbit
ラディッシュ	*radisshu*	radish
レーズン	*reezun*	raisin
レリッシュ	*rerisshu*	relish
ご飯	*gohan*	rice
煎餅	*senbee*	rice crackers
ロースト	*roosuto*	roast
ローストビーフ	*roosuto biifu*	roast beef
ロールパン	*rooru pan*	roll
ラム酒	*ramu shu*	rum
サラダ	*sarada*	salad
サラミ	*sarami*	salami
鮭(サケ)	*sake*	salmon
いくら	*ikura*	salmon roe

塩 *shio*	salt
サンドイッチ *sandoitchi*	sandwich
イワシ *iwashi*	sardine
ソース *soosu*	sauce
ソーセージ *sooseeji*	sausage
お好み焼き *okonomiyaki*	savory pancakes
ねぎ *negi*	scallion [spring onion]
帆立貝 *hotate gai*	scallop
スコッチ *sukotchi*	scotch
魚介類/海鮮料理 *gyokai rui/kaisen ryoori*	seafood
海苔 *nori*	seaweed (dried)
シェリー *sherii*	sherry
椎茸(しいたけ) *shiitake*	shitake mushroom
海老 *ebi*	shrimp [prawns]
炭酸飲料 *tansan inryoo*	soda
ソーダ *sooda*	soda water
スープ *suupu*	soup

醤油	soy (sauce)
shooyu	
スパゲッティ	spaghetti
supagetti	
ほうれん草	spinach
hoorensoo	
かぼちゃ	squash
kabocha	
いか	squid
ika	
ステーキ	steak
suteeki	
苺(いちご)	strawberry
ichigo	
砂糖	sugar
satoo	
甘いもの	sweets
amaimono	
サツマイモ	sweet potato
satsumaimo	
メカジキ	swordfish
mekajiki	
シロップ	syrup
shiroppu	
蜜柑(みかん)	tangerine
mikan	
タラゴン	tarragon
taragon	
紅茶	tea (black)
koocha	
トースト	toast
toosuto	
タイム	thyme
taimu	

豆腐 *toofu*	tofu (soybean curd)
トマト *tomato*	tomato
トニック *tonikku*	tonic water
胃袋 *ibukuro*	tripe
鱒(マス) *masu*	trout
トリュフ *toryufu*	truffles
鮪(マグロ) *maguro*	tuna
七面鳥 *shichimenchoo*	turkey
かぶ *kabu*	turnip
バニラ *banira*	vanilla
子牛の肉 *koushinoniku*	veal
野菜 *yasai*	vegetable
鹿の肉 *shika no niku*	venison
ベルモット *berumotto*	vermouth
ウォッカ *wokka*	vodka
酢 *su*	vinegar
水 *mizu*	water

クレソン *kureson*	watercress
西瓜(すいか) *suika*	watermelon
小麦 *komugi*	wheat
うどん *udon*	wheat noodles
ウイスキー *uisukii*	whisky
大根 *daikon*	white radish
白子(シラス) *shirasu*	whitebait
猪 *inoshishi*	wild boar
ワイン *wain*	wine
ヨーグルト *yooguruto*	yogurt
ズッキーニ *zukkiini*	zucchini [courgette]

PEOPLE

GOING OUT

NEED TO KNOW

What is there to do in the evenings?	夜は 何がありますか。 *yoru wa nani ga arimasu ka*
Do you have a program of events?	催し物のプログラムがありますか。 *moyooshimono no puroguramu gaarimasu ka*
What's playing at the movies [cinema] tonight?	今晩、どんな映画をやっていますか。 *konban donna eega o yatte imasu ka*
Where's...?	…はどこですか。 *...wa doko desu ka*
the downtown area	繁華街 *hankagai*
the bar	バー *baa*
the dance club	ディスコ *disuko*
Is there a cover charge?	カバーチャージはありますか。 *kabaa chaaji wa arimasu ka*

ENTERTAINMENT

Can you recommend...?	…はありますか。
	...wa arimasu ka
a concert	コンサート
	konsaato
a movie	映画
	eega
an opera	オペラ
	opera
a play	芝居
	shibai
When does it start/ end?	いつ始まりますか/終わりますか。
	itsu hajimarimasu ka/owarimasu ka
What's the dress code?	服装規定がありますか。
	fukusoo kitei ga arimasu ka
I like …	…が好きです。
	...ga suki desu
classical music	クラシック音楽
	kurashikku ongaku
folk music	フォーク
	fooku
jazz	ジャズ
	jazu

If you are looking for popular music and dancing you'll find good quality jazz clubs and conventional discos, even country and- western bars, all in Tokyo's cosmopolitan restaurant districts of Akasaka and Roppongi. Teenagers might like to join in the open-air dancing at Harajuku, near Yoyogi Park.

ⓘ

There are many local and regional festivals throughout the year in Japan. Some examples are; the Snow Festival in Sapporo, from late February to mid-March. In late March to early April the famous Japanese cherry blossoms invite everyone out to enjoy. In May, Kyoto has the Aoi Festival, one of three festivals that reenact Kyoto's history. The other two are the Jidai Festival in October and Gion Festival in July.

pop music	**ポピュラー音楽**	
	popyuraa ongaku	
rap	**ラップ音楽**	
	rappu ongaku	

NIGHTLIFE

What is there to do in the evenings?	**夜は何がありますか。**	
	yoru wa nani ga arimasu ka	
Can you recommend...?	**いい…はありますか。**	
	ii...wa arimasu ka	
a bar	**バー**	
	baa	
a dance club	**ディスコ**	
	disuko	
a gay club	**ゲイバー**	
	gee baa	
a jazz club	**ジャズクラブ**	
	jazu kurabu	
a karaoke bar	**カラオケバー**	
	karaoke baa	
a club with Japanese music	**日本の音楽が聴けるクラブ**	
	nihon no ongaku ga kikeru kurabu	

Is there live music?	生演奏がありますか。
	nama ensoo ga arimasu ka
How do I get there?	どうやって行くんですか。
	dooyatte ikun desu ka
Is there a cover charge?	カバーチャージはありますか。
	kabaa chaaji wa arimasu ka
Let's go dancing.	ダンスをしに行きましょう。
	dansu o shini ikimashoo
Is this area safe at night?	このあたりは、夜、安全ですか。
	kono atari wa yoru anzen desu ka

YOU MAY HEAR...

携帯電話をお切りください。
keitaidenwa o okiri kudasai

Turn off your cell [mobile] phones, please.

Japan has a wide variety of traditional arts and culture. Some examples from nature are: **bonsai**, an art to recreate nature on a small scale using plants; Japanese gardens, peaceful natural scenes located in cities or temples and **ikebana** or flower arrangement. If you prefer performances, don't miss **bunraku**, puppet theater using dolls of about three feet tall, manipulated by people on the stage. And of course there is **kabuki**, traditional Japanese theater.

ROMANCE

NEED TO KNOW

Would you like to go out for a drink/meal?	飲み物/食事はいかがですか。 *nomimono/shokuji wa ikaga desu ka*
What are your plans for tonight/tomorrow?	今晩/明日予定はありますか。 *konban/ashita yotee wa arimasu ka*
Can I have your number?	電話番号を教えてくれませんか。 *denwa bangoo o oshiete kuremasen ka*
Can I join you?	ご一緒してもいいですか。 *goissho shitemo ii desu ka*
Can I buy you a drink?	一杯おごらせてください。 *ippai ogorasete kudasai*
I like you.	あなたが気に入りました。 *anata ga kini irimashita*
I love you.	あなたが好きです。 *anata ga suki desu*

THE DATING GAME

Would you like to…?	行きませんか。
	…ikimasen ka
go out for coffee	コーヒーを飲みに
	koohii o nomi ni
go for a drink	飲みに
	nomi ni
go out for a meal	食事に
	shokuji ni
What are your for…?	…予定はありますか。
	…yotee wa arimasu ka
today	今日
	kyoo
tonight	今晩
	konban
tomorrow	明日
	ashita
this weekend	今週末
	konshuumatsu
Where would you like to go?	どこに行きましょうか。
	doko ni ikimashoo ka
I'd like to go to…	…に行きたいです。
	…ni ikitai desu
Do you like…?	…は好きですか。
	…wa suki desu ka
Can I have your number/e-mail?	電話番号/Eメールアドレスを教えてくれませんか。
	denwabangoo/iimeeru adoresu o oshiete kuremasen ka
Can I join you?	ご一緒してもいいですか。
	goissho shitemo ii desu ka
You're very attractive.	あなたはとても魅力的ですね。
	anata wa totemo miryokuteki desu ne

| Let's go somewhere quieter. | もっと静かなところへ行きましょう。 |
| | *motto shizukana tokoro e ikimasshoo* |

For Communications, see page 84.

ACCEPTING & REJECTING

I'd love to.	喜んで
	yorokonde
Where should we meet?	どこで待ち合わせましょうか。
	doko de machiawasemashoo ka
I'll meet you at the bar/your hotel.	バー/ホテルで会いましょう。
	baa/hoteru de aimashoo
I'll come by at...	…に来ます。
	...ni kimasu
What's your address?	住所は？
	juusho wa
Thank you, but I'm busy.	申し訳ありませんが、約束があります。
	mooshiwake arimasen ga yakusoku ga arimasu
I'm not interested.	興味がありません。
	kyuoomi ga arimasen
Leave me alone.	構わないでください。
	kamawanaide kudasai

| Stop bothering me! | 邪魔するのはやめてください。 |
| | *jama suru nowa yamete kudasai* |

GETTING INTIMATE

Can I hug/kiss you?	抱き締めても/キスしてもいいですか。
	dakishimetemo/kisushitemo ii desu ka
Yes.	はい
	hai
No.	いいえ
	iie
Stop!	やめて!
	yamete

SEXUAL PREFERENCES

Are you gay?	あなたはゲイですか。
	anata wa gee desu ka
I'm…	私は…です。
	watashi wa …desu
heterosexual	ヘテロ
	hetero
homosexual	ホモ
	homo
bisexual	バイ
	bai
Do you like men/ women ?	男性/女性が好きですか。
	dansei/josei ga suki desu ka

For Grammar, see page 14.

DICTIONARY

ENGLISH–JAPANESE

A

a.m. 午前 gozen
abbey 修道院 shuudooin
access v (Internet) アクセスします akusesu shimasu
accident 事故 jiko
accommodation 宿泊設備 shukuhaku setsubi
account n 会計 kaikee
acupuncture 鍼 hari
adapter アダプタ adaputa
address 住所 juusho
after …の後 …no ato
afternoon 午後 gogo
aftershave アフターシェーブ afutaa sheebu
age 年齢 nenree
agency 代理店 dairiten
AIDS エイズ eezu
air conditioning エアコン eakon
air pump エアポンプ eaponpu
airline 航空会社 kookuu gaisha
airmail 航空便 kookuubin
airplane 飛行機 hikooki
airport 空港 kuukoo
aisle 通路 tsuuro

aisle seat 通路側の座席 tsuurogawa no zaseki
allergic アレルギー arerugii
allergic reaction アレルギー反応 arerugii hannoo
alone 一人の人 hitori no hito
alter v (clothing) 直します naoshi masu
alternate route 他の道 hoka no michi
aluminum foil アルミホイル arumi hoiru
amazing すごい sugoi
ambulance 救急車 kyuukyuusha
American アメリカの amerika no
amusement park 遊園地 yuuenchi
anemic 貧血の hinketsu no
anesthesia 麻酔 masui
animal 動物 doobutsu
ankle 足首 ashikubi
antibiotic 抗生物質 koosee busshitsu
antiques store 骨董店 kottooten

adj adjective	**BE** British English	**prep** preposition
adv adverb	**n** noun	**v** verb

antiseptic cream 傷薬 kizugusuri

anything 何でも nandemo

apartment マンション manshon

appendix (body part) 盲腸 moochoo

appetizer おつまみ otsumami

appointment 予約 yoyaku

arcade アーケード aakeedo

area code 市外局番 shigai kyokuban

arm 腕 ude

aromatherapy アロマセラピー aroma serapii

around (the corner) 道を曲がったところ michi o magatta tokoro

arrivals (airport) 到着 toochaku

arrive v 着きます tsuki masu

artery 動脈 doomyaku

arthritis 関節炎 kansetsuen

Asian アジアの ajia no

aspirin 頭痛薬 zutsuuyaku

asthmatic 喘息の zensoku no

ATM キャッシュコーナー kyasshu koonaa

attack v 襲います osoimasu

attend v 出席します shusseki shimasu

attraction (place) アトラクション atorakushon

attractive 魅力的 miryokuteki

Australian オーストラリア人 oosutorariajin

automatic 自動 jidoo

automatic car オートマチック ootomachikku

B

baby 赤ちゃん akachan

baby bottle 哺乳瓶 honyuubin

baby wipe おしりふき oshirifuki

babysitter ベビーシッター bebii shittaa

back (body part) 背中 senaka

backpack リュックサック ryukkusakku

bag バッグ baggu

baggage [BE] 荷物 nimotsu

baggage claim 荷物引渡所 nimotsu hikiwatashijo

baggage ticket 荷物引換証 nimotsu hikikaeshoo

bakery パン屋 pan-ya

ballet バレエ baree

bandage 包帯 hootai

bank 銀行 ginkoo

bar バー baa

barber 床屋 tokoya

baseball 野球 yakyuu

basket (grocery store) かご kago

basketball バスケットボール basuketto booru

bathroom 風呂場 furoba

bathroom (toilet) トイレ toire

battery 電池 denchi

battleground 戦場跡 senjooato

beach 海岸/ビーチ kaigan/ biichi

beautiful 美しい utsukushii

bed ベッド beddo

begin v 始めます hajime masu

before 前 mae

beginner 初心者 shoshinsha

behind 後ろ ushiro

beige ベージュ beeju

belt ベルト beruto

berth 寝台 shindai

best 一番いい ichiban ii

better もっといい motto ii

bicycle 自転車 jitensha

big 大きい ookii

bigger もっと大きい motto ookii

bike route 自転車ルート jitensha ruuto

bikini ビキニ bikini

bill v (charge) 請求します seekyuu shimasu; ~ n (money) 紙幣 shihee; ~ n (of sale) 請求書 seekyuusho; itemized ~ 明細書 meesaisho

bird 鳥 tori

birthday 誕生日 tanjoobi

black 黒い kuroi

bladder 膀胱 bookoo

bland 味が薄い aji ga usui

blanket 毛布 moofu

bleed v 出血します shukketsu shimasu

blood 血液 ketsueki

blood pressure 血圧 ketsuatsu

blouse ブラウス burausu

blue ブルー buruu

board v (plane) 搭乗します toojoo shimasu, (train) 乗車 します joosha shimasu

boarding pass 搭乗券 toojoo ken

boat ボート booto

bone 骨 hone

book 本 hon

bookstore 本屋 hon-ya

boots ブーツ buutu

boring つまらない tsumaranai

botanical garden 植物園 shokubutsuen

bother v 邪魔します jama shimasu

bottle 瓶 bin

bottle opener 栓抜き sennuki

bowl ボール booru

box 箱 hako

boy 男の子 otoko noko

boyfriend ボーイフレンド booi furendo

bra ブラジャー burajaa

bracelet ブレスレット buresuretto

brakes (car) ブレーキ bureeki

break v 折れます oremasu

break-in (burglary) 侵入します shinnyuu shimasu

breakdown 故障 koshoo

breakfast 朝食 chooshoku

breast 乳房 chibusa

breastfeed 母乳をあげます bonyuu o agemasu

breathe v 呼吸します kokyuu shimasu

bridge 橋 hashi

briefs (clothing) ブリーフ buriifu

bring (people) v 連れてきます tsurete kimasu; **(things)** 持ってきます motte kimasu

British イギリス人 igirisujin

broken 壊れた kowareta

brooch ブローチ buroochi

broom 箒 hooki

brother (my older) 兄 ani

brother (my younger) 弟 ototoo

brother (someone else's older) お兄さん oniisan

brother (someone else's younger) 弟さん otootosan

brown 茶色 chairo

bug 虫 mushi

building ビル/ 建物 biru/ tatemono

burn v 焼きます yakimasu

bus バス basu

bus station バスターミナル basu taaminaru

bus stop バス停留所 / バス停 basu teeryuujo/basutee

bus ticket バスの切符 basu no kippu

bus tour バス旅行 basu ryokoo

business 仕事 shigoto

business card 名刺 meeshi

business center ビジネス・センター bijinesu sentaa

business class ビジネス・クラス bijinesu kurasu

business hours 営業時間 eegyoo jikan

butcher 肉屋 nikuya

buttocks お尻 oshiri

buy v 買います kaimasu

bye ごめんください gomen kudasai

C

cabin キャビン kyabin

cable car ケーブル・カー keeburu kaa

café 喫茶店 kissaten

call v 電話します denwa shimasu

calligraphy supplies 習字用具 shuuji yoogu

calories カロリー karorii

camera カメラ kamera

camp v キャンプします kyanpu shimasu; **no ~ing** キャンプ禁止 kyanpu kinshi

campsite キャンプ場 kyanpujoo

can opener 缶切り kankiri
Canada カナダ kanada
Canadian カナダ人 kanadajin
cancel v キャンセルします kyanseru shimasu
candy キャンデー kyandee
canned good 缶詰 kanzume
canyon 峡谷 kyookoku
car 車 kuruma
car hire [BE] レンタカー rentakaa
car park [BE] 駐車場 chuushajoo
car rental レンタカー rentakaa
car seat チャイルドシート chairudo shiito
carafe カラフ karafu
card カード kaado
carry-on 手荷物 tenimotsu
cart カート kaato
carton カートン kaaton
case (amount) ケース keesu
cash v 換金します kankin shimasu; ~ n 現金 genkin
cash advance キャッシング・サービス kyasshingu saabisu
cashier 会計 kaikee
casino カジノ kajino
castle お城 oshiro
cathedral 大聖堂 daiseedoo
cave 洞窟 dookutsu
CD CD shii dii
cell phone 携帯電話 keetai denwa
Celsius 接氏 sesshi

centimeter センチメートル senchi-meetoru
chair 椅子 isu
chair lift スキーリフト sukii rifuto
change v (buses) 乗り換えます norikaemasu; ~ v (money) 替えます kaemasu; ~ v (baby) おむつを替えます omutsu o kaemasu; ~ n (plan) 変更 henkoo; ~ n (money) お釣り otsuri
charcoal 炭 sumi
charge v (credit card) カードで払います kaado de haraimasu; n (cost) 料金 ryookin
cheap 安い yasui
cheaper もっと安い motto yasui
check v (something) 調べます shirabemasu; ~ v (luggage) 預けます azukemasu; ~ n (payment) お勘定 okanjoo
check-in チェックイン chekku in
checking account 当座預金口座 tooza yoking kooza
check-out (hotel) n チェックアウト chekku auto
chemical toilet ケミカルトイレ kemikaru toire
chemist [BE] 薬局 yakkyoku
cheque [BE] チェック chekku
chest (body part) 胸 mune

chest pain 胸の痛み mune no itami

chewing gum ガム gamu

child 子供 kodomo

child's seat 子供用の椅子 kodomoyoo no isu

children's menu 子供用のメニュー kodomoyoo no menyuu

children's portion 子供用のメニュー kodomoyoo no menyuu

china 瀬戸物 setomono

China 中国 chuugoku

Chinese (language) 中国語 chuugokugo

Chinese (people) 中国人 chuugokujin

chopsticks おはし ohashi

church 教会 kyookai

cigar 葉巻 hamaki

cigarette 煙草 tabako

class クラス kurasu

clay pot 土器 doki

classical music クラシック音楽 kurashikku ongaku

clean v きれいにします kirei ni shimasu; ~ adj きれい kiree

cleaning product 洗浄剤 senjoozai

cleaning supplies クリーニング用品 kuriiningu yoohin

clear v (on an ATM) 消去します shookyo shimasu

cliff 崖 gake

cling film [BE] ラップ rappu

close v (a shop) 閉めます shimemasu; ~ adj 近い chikai

closed 閉館 heekan

clothing 衣類 irui

clothing store 洋服屋 yoofukuya

club クラブ kurabu

coat コート kooto

coffee shop 喫茶店 kissaten

coin 硬貨 kooka

cold (sickness) 風邪 kaze; ~ (weather) 寒い samui; ~ (food) 冷たい tsumetai

colleague 同僚 dooryoo

cologne オーデコロン oodekoron

color 色 iro

comb 櫛 kushi

come v 来ます kimasu

complaint 苦情 kujoo

computer コンピュータ konpyuuta

concert コンサート konsaato

concert hall コンサートホール konsaato hooru

condition (medical) 症状 shoojoo

conditioner コンディショナー kondishonaa

condom コンドーム kondoomu

conference 会議 kaigi

confirm v 確認します kakunin shimasu

congestion 混雑 konzatsu

connect v (internet) 接続しま
す setsuzoku shimasu
connection (internet) 接続
setsuzoku; **~ (flight)** 連絡
renraku
constipated 便秘 benpi
consulate 領事館 ryoojikan
consultant コンサルタント
konsarutanto
contact v 連絡します renraku
shimasu
contact lens コンタクトレンズ
kontakuto renzu;
~ solution コンタクトレンズ液
kontakuto renzu eki
contagious 伝染性 densensee
convention hall 会議場
kaigijoo
conveyor belt コンベヤーベル
ト konbeyaa beruto
cook v 料理します ryoori
shimasu
cooking gas ガス gasu
cool (temperature) 涼しい
suzushii
copper 銅 doo
corkscrew コルクスクリュー
koruku sukuryuu
cost v かかります kakarimasu
cot 折り畳みベッド oritatami
beddo
cotton 綿／コットン men/
kotton
cough 咳 seki

country code 国番号 kuni
bangoo
cover charge カバーチャージ
kabaa chaaji
crash v (car) ぶつかります
butsukarimasu
cream (ointment) 軟膏
nankoo
credit card クレジットカード
kurejitto kaado
crew neck クルーネック kuruu
nekku
crib ベビーベッド bebii beddo
crystal 水晶 suishoo
cup カップ kappu
currency 通貨 tsuuka
currency exchange 両替
ryoogae; **~ office** 両替所
ryoogaejo
current account [BE] 当座預
金 tooza yokin
customs 税関 zeekan
cut v (hair) カットします katto
shimasu
cut n (injury) 傷 kizu
cute 可愛い kawaii
cycling サイクリング saikuringu

D

damage v 壊れます
kowaremasu
damaged 壊れた kowareta
dance v 踊ります odorimasu
dance club ダンスクラブ
dansu kurabu

dangerous 危ない abunai

dark 暗い kurai

date (calendar) 日付け hizuke

day 日 hi

deaf 耳が聞こえない mimi ga kikoenai

debit card デビットカード debitto kaado

deck chair デッキチェア dekki chea

declare v 申告します shisnkoku shimasu

decline v (credit card) 拒否します kyohi shimasu

deeply 深く fukaku

degrees (temperature) 度 do

delay v 遅れます okuremasu

delete v 削除します sakujo shimasu

delicatessen デリカテッセン derikatessen

delicious おいしい oishii

denim デニム denimu

dentist 歯医者 haisha

denture 入れ歯 ireba

deodorant デオドラント deodoranto

department store デパート depaato

departure 出発 shuppatsu

deposit v 預けます azukemasu; ~ n (security) 前金 maekin

desert 砂漠 sabaku

detergent 洗剤 senzai

diabetic 糖尿病 toonyoobyoo

dial v 電話をかけます denwa o kakemasu

diamond ダイアモンド daiamondo

diaper おむつ omutsu

diarrhea 下痢 geri

diesel ディーゼル diizeru

difficult 難しい muzukashii

digital デジタル dejitaru; ~ camera デジタルカメラ dejitaru kamera; ~ photo デジタル写真 dejitaru shashin; ~ print デジタルカメラプリント dejitaru kamera purinto

dining room 食堂 shokudoo

dinner 食事 shokuji

direction 方向 hookoo

dirty 汚い kitanai

disabled 身体障害者 shintai shoogaisha; ~ accessible [BE] バリアフリー設備 baria furii setsubi

disconnect (computer) 接続を切ります setsuzoku o kirimasu

discount 割引 waribiki

dish (kitchen) 食器 shokki

dishwasher 食洗器 shokusen ki

dishwashing liquid 中性洗剤 chuusee senzai

display 表示 hyooji

display case ショーケース shookeesu

disposable 使い捨て tsukaisute

disposable razor 使い捨てカミソリ tsukaisute kamisori

dive v 飛び込みます tobikomimasu

diving equipment 潜水用具 sensui yoogu

divorce v 離婚します rikon shimasu

dizzy めまいがします memai ga shimasu

doctor 医者 isha

doll 人形 ningyoo

dollar (U.S.) ドル doru

domestic 国内の kokunai no

domestic flight 国内線 kokunaisen

dormitory 寮 ryoo

double bed ダブルベッド daburu beddo

downtown 繁華街 hankagai

dozen ダース daasu

drag lift 抗力浮揚 kooryoku fuyoo

dress (piece of clothing) ワンピース wanpiisu

dress code 服装規定 fukusoo kitee

drink v 飲みます nomimasu; ~ n 飲み物 nomimono

drink menu ドリンクメニュー dorinku menyuu

drinking water 飲料水 inryoosui

drive v 運転します unten shimasu

driver's license 運転免許証 unten menkyoshoo; ~ **number** 運転免許証番号 unten menkyoshoo bangoo

drop (medicine) 一滴 itteki

drowsiness 眠気 nemuke

dry cleaner ドライクリーニング店 dorai kuriiningu ten

during …の間 …no aida

duty (tax) 関税 kanzee

duty-free 免税 menzee

DVD DVD dii bui dii

E

ear 耳 mimi

earache 耳の痛み mimi no itami

early 早い hayai

earrings イヤリング iyaringu

east 東 higashi

easy やさしい yasashii

eat v 食べます tabeamasu

economy class エコノミークラス ekonomii kurasu

elbow 肘 hiji

electric outlet コンセント konsento

elevator エレベーター erebeetaa

e-mail v メールします meeru shimasu; ~ n 電子メール denshi meeru

e-mail address 電子メールアドレス denshi meeru adoresu

emergency 緊急 kinkyuu

emergency exit 非常口 hijoo guchi

empty v 空にします kara ni shimasu

end v 終わります owarimasu

English (language) 英語 eego

English (people) イギリス人 igirisujin

engrave v 彫り込みます horikomimasu

enjoy v 楽しみます tanoshimimasu

enter v 入ります hairimasu; (computer) 入力します nyuuryoku shimasu

entertainment エンターテインメント entaateenmento

entrance 入口 iriguchi

envelope 封筒 fuutoo

equipment 道具 doogu

escalator エスカレーター esukareetaa

e-ticket Eチケット i chiketto

evening 夕方 yuugata

excess 超過 chooka

exchange v (money) 両替します ryoogae shimasu; ~ v (goods) 取り替えます torikaemasu; ~ n (place) 交換所 kookanjo

exchange rate (為替)レート (kawase) reeto

excursion エクスカーション ekusukaashon

excuse v 許します yurushimasu

exhausted 疲れている tsukareteiru

exit v 出ます demasu; ~ n 出口 deguchi

expensive 高い takai

expert (skill level) 専門家 senmonka

exposure (film) …枚撮り… maitori

express (mail) 速達 sokutatsu; (train) 急行 kyuukoo

extension (phone) 内線 naisen

extra 特別な tokubetsuna

extra large 特大 tokudai

extract v (tooth) 抜きます nukimasu

eye 目 me

F

face 顔 kao

facial フェーシャル feesharu

family 家族 kazoku

fan (appliance) 扇風機 senpuuki

far 遠い tooi

far-sighted 遠視の enshi no

farm 農家 nooka

fast 速い hayai

fast food ファーストフード faasuto fuudo

fat free 無脂肪 mushiboo

father (one's own) 父 chichi; (someone else's) お父さん otoosan

fax v ファックスします fakkusu shimasu; ~ n ファックス fakkusu

fax number ファックス番号 fakkusu bangoo

fee 費用 hiyoo

feed v 授乳します junyuu shimasu

ferry フェリー ferii

fever 熱 netsu

field (sports) フィールド fiirudo

fill up v (food) 満タンにします mantan ni shimasu

fill out v (form) 記入します kinyuu shimasu

filling (tooth) 詰物 tsumemono

film (camera) フイルム fuirumu

fine (fee) 罰金 bakkin

finger 指 yubi

fingernail 爪 tsume

fire 火 hi

fire department 消防署 shooboosho

fire door 耐火扉 taika tobira

first 最初の saisho no

first class ファーストクラス faasuto kurasu

fish 魚 sakana

fit (clothing) 合います aimasu

fitting room 試着室 shichakushitsu

fix v (repair) 直します naoshi masu

flashlight 懐中電灯 kaichuu dentoo

flight 便 bin

floor 階 kai

flower 花 hana

folk music フォークミュージック fooku myuujikku

food 食物 tabemono

foot 足 ashi

football game [BE] サッカーゲーム sakkaa geemu

for (a day) 一日間 ichiinichiikan

forecast 予報 yohoo

foreigner 外国人 gaikokujin

forest 森 mori

fork フォーク fooku

form (fill-in) 用紙 yooshi

formula (baby) フォーミュラ foomyura

fountain 噴水 funsui

free (not busy) 暇 hima; ~ (available) 空いています aiteimasu;

free (no charge) 無料 muryoo

freezer 冷凍庫 reetooko

fresh 新しい atarashii

friend 友人 yuujin

frying pan フライパン furaipan

full-service 完全サービス kanzen saabisu

G

game ゲーム geemu
garage 修理工場 shuurikoojoo
garbage bag ごみ袋 gomibukuro
gas ガソリン gasorin
gas station ガソリンスタンド gasorin sutando
gate (airport) ゲート geeto
gay bar ゲイバー gei baa
gay club ゲイクラブ gei kurabu
gel (hair) ジェル jeru
get to 着きます tsukimasu
get off (a train/bus/subway) 下ります orimasu
gift 贈り物 okurimono
gift shop 売店 baiten
girl 女の子 onna no ko
girlfriend ガールフレンド gaaru furendo
give v あげます agemasu
glass (drinking) コップ koppu; ~ **(material)** ガラス garasu
glasses 眼鏡 megane
go v **(somewhere)** 行きます ikimasu
gold 金 kin
golf course ゴルフ場 gorufujoo
golf tournament ゴルフトーナメント gorufu toonamento
good 良い ii; **(food)** おいしい oishii

good afternoon こんにちは konnichiwa
good evening 今晩は konbanwa
good morning お早うございます ohayoo gozaimasu
goodbye さようなら sayoonara
gram グラム guramu
grandchild 孫 mago
grandparent (one's own) 祖父/祖母 sofu/sobo; **(someone else's)** おじいさん／おばあさん ojiisan/obaasan
gray グレー guree
green 緑／グリーン midori/guriin
grocery store 食料品店 shokuryoohinten
ground floor 一階 ikkai
group グループ guruupu
guide n ガイド gaido
guide book ガイドブック gaido bukku
guide dog 盲導犬 moodoo ken
gym トレーニングジム toreeningu jimu
gynecologist 婦人科医 fujinkai

H

hair 髪 kami
hair dryer ヘアドライヤー hea doraiyaa
hair salon 美容院 biyooin

hairbrush ヘアブラシ hea burashi

haircut ヘアカット hea katto

hairspray ヘアスプレー hea supuree

hairstyle ヘアスタイル hea sutairu

hairstylist ヘアスタイリスト hea sutairisuto

half 半分 hanbun

half hour 半時間 han jikan

half-kilo 半キロ han kiro

hammer ハンマー hanmaa

hand 手 te

hand luggage [BE] 手荷物 tenimotsu

handbag [BE] ハンドバッグ hando baggu

handicapped 身体障害者 shintai shoogaisha

handicapped-accessible ハンディキャップ用 handikyappuyoo

hangover 二日酔い futsuka yoi

happy 楽しい tanoshii

hat 帽子 booshi

have v あります arimasu

head (body part) 頭 atama

headache 頭痛 zutsuu

headphones ヘッドフォン heddofon

health 健康 kenkoo

health food store 健康食品店 kenkoo shokuhinten

heart 心臓 shinzoo

heart condition 心臓病 shinzoobyoo

heat 熱 netsu

heater 暖房 danboo

heating [BE] ヒーター／暖房 hiitaa/danboo

hello こんにちは konnichiwa; **(on the phone)** もしもし moshi moshi

helme ヘルメット herumetto

help 助け tasuke

here ここ koko

hi どうも doomo

high 高い takai

highchair ハイチェアー haicheaa

highway ハイウェー haiuee

hill 丘 oka

hire v [BE] 借ります karimasu

hire car [BE] レンタカー rentakaa

hitchhike v ヒッチハイクします hitchi haiku shimasu

hockey ホッケー hokkee

holiday [BE] 休日 kyuujitsu

horse track 競馬場 keebajoo

hospital 病院 byooin

hostel ホステル hosuteru

hot (temperature) 暑い atsui; **~ (spicy)** 辛い karai

hot spring 温泉 onsen

hot water お湯 oyu

hotel ホテル hoteru

hour 時間 jikan

house 家 ie

household good 家庭用品 katee yoohin

housekeeping services 客室清掃サービス kyakushitsu seesoo saabisu

how どうやって dooyatte

how much (money) いくら ikura; **(quantity)** どのくらい dono kurai

hungry お腹がすいた onaka ga suita

hurt 痛い itai

husband (one's own) 主人 shujin; **(some one else's)** ご主人 goshujin

I

ibuprofen イブプロフェン ibupurofen

ice 氷 koori

ice hockey アイスホッケー aisu hokkee

icy 氷の koori no

identification 身分証明 mibun shoomee

ill 病気 byooki

include v 含みます fukumimasu

indoor pool 室内プール shitsunai puuru

inexpensive 安い yasui

infected 感染した kansen shita

information (phone) 案内 annai

information desk 受付 uketsuke

inn 旅館 ryokan

insect bite 虫さされ mushi sasare

insect repellent 虫除け mushi yoke

insert v **(on an ATM)** 挿入します／入れます soonyuu shimasu/iremasu

insomnia 不眠症 fuminshoo

instant message インスタント・メッセージ insutanto messeeji

insulin インスリン insurin

insurance 保険 hoken; v 保険を掛けます hoken o kakemasu

insurance card 保険証 hokenshoo

insurance company 保険会社 hoken gaisha

interesting 面白い omoshiroi

international (airport area) 国際 kokusai

international flight 国際線 kokusaisen

international student card 国際学生証 kokusai gakuseishoo

internet インターネット intaanetto

internet cafe インターネットカフェ intaanetto kafe
internet service インターネットサービス intaanetto saabisu
interpreter 通訳者 tsuuyakusha
intersection 交差点 koosaten
intestine 腸 choo
introduce v 紹介します shookai shimasu
invoice 請求書 seekyuusho
Ireland アイルランド airurando
Irish アイルランド人 airurando jin
iron v アイロンをかけます airon o kakemasu; ~ n アイロン airon

J

jacket ジャケット jaketto
Japanese (people) 日本人 nihonjin
Japanese (language) 日本語 nihongo
jar 瓶 bin
jaw 顎 ago
jazz ジャズ jazu
jazz club ジャズクラブ jazu kurabu
jeans ジーパン／ジーンズ jiipan/jiinzu
jeweler 宝石店 hoosekiten
jewelry 宝石 hooseki

join v 加入します kanyuu shimasu
joint (body part) 関節 kansetsu

K

key 鍵 kagi
key card キーカード kii kaado
key ring キーホルダー kii horudaa
kiddie pool 子供用プール kodomoyoo puuru
kidney (body part) 腎臓 jinzoo
kilogram キロ(グラム) kiro (guramu)
kilometer キロ(メートル) kiro (meetoru)
kiss v キスします kisu shimasu
kitchen 台所 daidokoro; ~ foil [BE] アルミフォイル arumifoiru
knee 膝 hiza
knife ナイフ naifu

L

lace レース reesu
lacquerware 漆器 shikki
lactose intolerant 乳糖不耐症 nyuutoo futaishoo
lake 湖 mizuumi
large 大きい ookii
last 最後 saigo
late (time) 遅い osoi
later あとで atode

launderette [BE] コインランド
リー koin randorii
laundromat コインランドリー
koin randorii
laundry 洗濯 sentaku
laundry facility 洗濯施設
sentaku shisetsu
laundry service ランドリーサ
ービス randorii saabisu
lawyer 弁護士 bengoshi
leather 皮 kawa
leave v 出ます demasu
left (direction) 左 hidari
leg 脚 ashi
lens レンズ renzu
less もっと少ない motto
sukunai
lesson レッスン ressun
letter 手紙 tegami
library 図書館 toshokan
life boat 救命ボート kyuumee
booto
life jacket 救命胴衣 kyuumee
dooi
lifeguard ライフガード raifu
gaado
lift リフト rifuto; ~ [BE] エレベー
ター erebeetaa
lift pass リフト券 rifuto ken
light (overhead) 電灯 dentoo;
~ v **(cigarette)** 火をつけます
hi o tsukemasu
lightbulb 電球 denkyuu
lighter ライター raitaa
like v 好きです sukidesu

line (train) 線 sen
linen 麻 asa
lip 唇 kuchibiru
liquor store 酒屋 sakaya
liter リットル rittoru
little 少し／ちょっと sukoshi/
chotto
live v 住みます sumimasu
liver (body part) 肝臓 kanzoo
loafers ローファー roofaa
local 地方 chihoo
lock v 鍵をかけます kagi o
kakemasu; ~ n 鍵 kagi
locker ロッカー rokkaa
log on ログオンします roggu on
shimasu
log off ログオフします roggu
ofu shimasu
long 長い nagai
long sleeves 長袖 nagasode
long-sighted [BE] 遠視 enshi
look v 見ます mimasu
lose v **(something)** なくします
nakushimasu
lost 道に迷いました michi ni
mayoi mashita
lost and found お忘れ物
承り所 owasure mono
uketamawari jo
lotion ローション rooshon
louder もっと大きい声で motto
ookii koe de
love 愛 ai
low 低い hikui
luggage 荷物 nimotsu

luggage cart カート kaato

luggage locker コインロッカー koin rokkaa

luggage ticket 荷物引換券 nimotsu hikikae ken

lunch 昼食 chuushoku

lung 肺 hai

M

magazine 雑誌 zasshi

magnificent 立派 rippa

mail v 郵送します yuusoo shimasu; ~ n 手紙 tegami

mailbox 郵便ポスト yuubin posuto

main attraction メインイベント mein ibento

main course メインコース mein koosu

make up a prescription [BE] 調合します choogoo shimasu

mall ショッピングモール shoppingu mooru

man 男の人 otoko no hito

manager (restaurant, hotel) 支配人 shihainin; (shop) 店長 tenchoo

manicure マニキュア manikyua

manual car マニュアル manyuaru

map n 地図 chizu

market マーケット maaketto

married 結婚している kekkon shiteiru

marry v 結婚します kekkon shimasu

mass (church service) ミサ misa

massage マッサージ massaaji

match n 試合 shiai

meal 食事 shokuji

measure v (someone) 測ります hakarimasu

measuring cup 計量カップ keeryoo kappu

measuring spoon 計量スプーン keeryoo supuun

mechanic 修理工 shuurikoo

medicine 薬 kusuri

medium (size) 中ぐらい chuugurai

meet v (someone) 待ち合わせす machiawasemasu

meeting 会議 kaigi

meeting room 会議室 kaigishitsu

membership card 会員証 kaiin shoo

memorial (place) 記念館 kinenkan

memory card メモリーカード memorii kaado

mend v 直します naoshimasu

menstrual cramp 生理痛 seiritsuu

menu メニュー menyuu

message メッセージ、ご伝言 messeeji, godengon

meter (parking) 料金メーター ryookin meetaa

microwave 電子レンジ denshi renji

midday [BE] 昼間 hiruma

midnight 真夜中 mayonaka

mileage 距離 kyori

mini-bar ミニバー mini baa

minute 分 fun/pun

missing いなくなる inakunaru

mistake 間違い machigai

mobile phone [BE] 携帯電話 keetai denwa

mobility 移動性 idoosee

money お金 okane

month 月 tsuki

mop モップ moppu

moped モペット mopetto

more もっと motto

morning 朝 asa

mosque 回教寺院 kaikyoo jiin

mother (one's own) 母 haha; (some one else's) お母さん okaasan

motion sickness 乗物酔い norimono yoi

motor boat モーターボート mootaa booto

motorcycle オートバイ ootobai

motorway [BE] 高速道路 koosoku dooro

mountain 山 yama

mountain bike マウンテンバイク maunten baiku

mousse (hair) ムース muusu

mouth 口 kuchi

movie 映画 eega

movie theater 映画館 eegakan

mug v 襲います osoimasu

muscle 筋肉 kinniku

museum 博物館 hakubutsukan

music 音楽 ongaku

music store 楽器屋 gakkiya

N

nail file ネイルファイル neeru fairu

nail salon ネイルサロン neeru saron

name 名前 namae

napkin ナプキン napukin

nappy [BE] おむつ omutsu

nationality 国籍 kokuseki

nature preserve 自然保護区 shizen hogoku

nauseous 吐き気 hakike

near 近く chikaku

near-sighted 近視 kinshi

nearby 近く chikaku

neck 首 kubi

necklace ネックレス nekkuresu

need v 要ります irimasu

newspaper 新聞 shinbun

newsstand キオスク kiosuku

next 次 tsugi

nice すてき suteki

night 夜 yoru

nightclub ナイトクラブ naito kurabu

no いいえ iie

non-alcoholic ノンアルコール non arukooru

non-smoking 禁煙 kin-en

noon 正午 shoogo

north 北 kita

nose 鼻 hana

note [BE] お札 osatsu

notify v 知らせます shirasemasu

novice (skill level) 初心者 shoshinsha

now 今 ima

number 数字 suuji

nurse 看護士 kangoshi

O

office オフィス ofisu

office hours オフィスアワー ofisu awaa

off-licence [BE] 酒屋 sakaya

oil オイル oiru

OK オーケー ookee

old (person) 年寄り toshiyori; **(thing)** 古い furui

on the corner 角の kadono

once 一度 ichido

one 一つ hitotsu

one-way (ticket) 片道 katamichi

one-way street 一方通行 ippoo tsuukoo

only ただ tada

open v 開けます akemasu; ~ adj 開いている aiteiru

opera オペラ opera

opera house オペラハウス opera hausu

opposite 向かい mukai

optician 眼鏡店 meganeten

orange (color) オレンジ色 orenji iro

orchestra オーケストラ ookesutora

order v 注文します chuumon shimasu

outdoor pool 屋外プール okugai puuru

outside 外 soto

over the counter (medication) 処方箋無し shohoosen nashi

overdone 焼き過ぎ yakisugi

overlook (scenic place) 見晴し台 miharashidai

overnight 夜通し yodooshi

oxygen treatment 酸素治療 sanso chiryoo

P

p.m. n 午後 gogo (1 p.m.; gogo ichiji)

pacifier おしゃぶり oshaburi

pack v 詰めます tsumemasu

package 小包 kozutsumi

paddling pool [BE] 子供用プール kodomoyoo puuru

pad [BE] 生理用ナプキン
seeriyoo napukin

pain 痛み itami

pajamas パジャマ pajama

palace 宮殿 kyuuden

pants ズボン zubon

pantyhose パンスト pansuto

paper 紙 kami

paper towel ペーパータオル
peepaa taoru

paracetamol [BE] アセタミノー
フェン asetaminoofen

park v 駐車します chuusha
shimasu; ~ n 公園 kooen

parking garage 駐車場
chuushajoo

parking lot 駐車場 chuushajoo

parking meter 料金メーター
ryookin meetaa

part (for car) 部品 buhin

part-time パートタイム paato
taimu

passenger 乗客 jookyaku

passport パスポート
pasupooto

passport control 入国手続き
nyuukoku tetsuzuki

password パスワード pasu
waado

pastry shop ケーキ屋 keekiya

path 道路 dooro

pay v 払います haraimasu

pay phone 公衆電話 kooshuu
denwa

peak (of a mountain) 山頂
sanchoo

pearl 真珠 shinju

pedestrian 歩行者 hokoosha

pediatrician 小児科医
shoonikai

pedicure ペディキュア
pedikyua

pen ペン pen

penicillin ペニシリン penishirin

penis ペニス penisu

per につき nitsuki

per day 一日につき ichinichi
ni tsuki

per hour 一時間につき
ichijikan ni tsuki

per night 一晩につき hitoban
ni tsuki

per week 一週間につき
isshuukan ni tsuki

perfume 香水 koosui

period (menstrual) 生理 seeri;
~(of time) 期間 kikan

permit v 許可します kyoka
shimasu

petite ペティート petiito

petrol [BE] ガソリン gasorin

petrol station [BE] ガソリンス
タンド gasorin sutando

pharmacy 薬局 yakkyoku

phone v 電話します denwa
shimasu; ~ n 電話 denwa

phone call 電話 denwa

phone card テレホンカード
terehon kaado

phone number 電話番号 denwa bangoo

photo 写真 shashin

photocopy コピー kopii

photography 写真撮影 shashin satsuee

pick up (something) 受け取ります uketorimasu

picnic area ピクニック場 pikunikkujoo

pill (birth control) ピル piru

pillow 枕 makura

personal identification number (PIN) 暗証番号 anshoo bangoo

pink ピンク pinku

piste [BE] ゲレンデ gerende

piste map [BE] ゲレンデ地図 gerende chizu

pizzeria ピザ・レストラン piza resutoran

place v (a bet) 掛け金を払います kakekin o haraimasu; n 場所 basho

plane 飛行機 hikooki

plastic wrap ラップ rappu

plate 皿 sara

platform ホーム hoomu

platinum プラチナ purachina

play v します shimasu; ~ n (theatre) 芝居 shibai

playground 公園 kooen

playpen ベビーサークル bebii saakuru

please (asking for a favor) お願いします onegai shimasu; **(offering a favor)** どうぞ doozo

pleasure 楽しみ tanoshimi

plunger トイレの吸引具 toire no kyuuingu

plus size プラスサイズ purasu saizu

pocket ポケット poketto

poison 毒 doku

poles (skiing) ストック sutokku

police 警察 keesatsu

police report 警察の証明書 keesatsu no shoomeesho

police station 交番 kooban

pond 池 ike

pool プール puuru

pop music ポピュラー音楽 popyuraa ongaku

portion 部分 bubun

post [BE] 手紙 tegami

post office 郵便局 yuubinkyoku

postbox [BE] 郵便ポスト yuubin posuto

postcard 葉書 hagaki

pot 深鍋 fukanabe

pottery 陶器 tooki

pound (weight) ポンド pondo; ~ **(British sterling)** ポンド pondo

pregnant 妊娠 ninshin

prepaid phone プリペイド携帯 puripeedo keetai

prescribe v 処方します shohoo
　shimasu
prescription 処方箋
　shohoosen
press v (clothing) アイロンを
　かけます airon o kakemasu
price 値段 nedan
print v 印刷します insatsu
　shimasu
problem 問題 mondai
produce 食料品 shokuryoohin
produce store 食料品店
　shokuryoohinten
prohibit v 禁止します kinshi
　shimasu
pronounce v 発音します
　hatsuon shimasu
public 公共 kookyoo
pull v 引きます hikimasu
purple 紫 murasaki
purse 財布 saifu
push v 押します oshimasu
pushchair [BE] ベビーカー
　bebii kaa

Q

quality 質 shitsu
question 質問 shitsumon
quiet 静か shizuka

R

racetrack 競馬場 keebajoo
racket (sports) ラケット
　raketto
railway station [BE] 駅 eki

rain n 雨 ame
raincoat レインコート
　reinkooto
rainforest 雨林 urin
rainy 雨の ameno
rap (music) ラップ rappu
rape 強姦 gookan
rash 発疹 hasshin
razor blade カミソリの刃
　kamisori no ha
reach v 届きます todokimasu
ready 用意ができている yooi
　ga dekite iru
real 本物 honmono
receipt レシート／領収書
　reshiito/ryooshuusho
receive v 受け取ります
　uketorimasu
reception 受付 uketsuke
recharge v 充電します juuden
　shimasu
recommend v 推薦します
　suisen shimasu
recommendation 推薦 suisen
recycling リサイクリング
　risaikuringu
red 赤い akai
refrigerator 冷蔵庫 reezooko
region 地域 chiiki
registered mail 書留 kakitome
regular レギュラー regyuraa
relationship 関係 kankee
rent v 借ります karimasu
rental car レンタカー rentakaa

repair v 修理します shuuri shimasu

repeat v もう一度言います moo ichido iimasu

reservation 予約 yoyaku

reservation desk 予約窓口 yoyaku madoguchi

reserve v 予約します yoyaku shimasu

restaurant レストラン resutoran

restroom 化粧室 keshooshitsu

retired 退職した taishoku shita

return v 返します kaeshimasu; ~ n [BE] 往復 oofuku

rib (body part) 肋骨 rokkotsu

rice cooker 炊飯器 suihanki

right (direction) 右 migi

right of way 優先権 yuusenken

ring 指輪／リング yubiwa/ ringu

river 川 kawa

road map 道路地図 dooro chizu

rob v 盗みます nusumimasu

robbed 盗まれました nusumare mashita

romantic ロマンチック romanchikku

room 部屋 heya

room key 部屋の鍵 heya no kagi

room service ルームサービス ruumu saabisu

round-trip 往復 oofuku

route コース koosu

rowboat ボート booto

rubbish [BE] ゴミ gomi

rubbish bag [BE] ゴミ袋 gomi bukuro

ruins 遺跡 iseki

rush ラッシュ rasshu

S

sad 悲しい kanashii

safe (thing) 金庫 kinko; ~ (protected) 安全 anzen

sales tax 消費税 shoohizee

sandals サンダル sandaru

sanitary napkin 生理用ナプキン seeriyoo napukin

saucepan 鍋 nabe

sauna サウナ sauna

save v (on a computer) 保存します hozon shimasu

savings (account) 普通預金 futsuu yokin

scanner スキャナー sukyanaa

scarf スカーフ sukaafu

schedule v 予定に入れます yotee ni iremasu; ~ n 予定 yotee

school 学校 gakkoo

science 科学 kagaku

scissors はさみ hasami

sea 海 umi

seat 席 seki

security 警備 keebi

see v 見ます mimasu

self-service セルフサービス serufu saabisu

sell v 売ります urimasu

seminar セミナー seminaa

send v 送ります okurimasu

senior citizen 高齢者 kooreesha

separated (marriage) 別居 bekkyo

serious 真面目な majimena

service (in a restaurant) サービス saabisu

sexually transmitted disease (STD) 性病 seebyoo

shampoo シャンプー shanpuu

sharp 鋭い surudoi

shaving cream シェービングクリーム sheebingu kuriimu

sheet シーツ shiitsu

ship v (mail) 送ります okurimasu

shirt シャツ shatsu

shoe store 靴屋 kutsuya

shoes 靴 kutsu

shop v 買い物をします kaimono o shimasu

shopping 買い物 kaimono

shopping area 商店街 shooten gai

shopping centre [BE] ショッピングセンター shoppingu sentaa

shopping mall ショッピングモール shoppingu mooru

short 短い mijikai

short sleeves 半袖 hansode

shorts 半ズボン hanzubon

short-sighted [BE] 近視 kinshi

shoulder 肩 kata

show v 見せます misemasu

shower シャワー shawaa

shrine 神社 jinja

sick 病気 byooki

side dish 付け合わせ tsukeawase

side effect 副作用 fukusayoo

sightseeing 観光 kankoo

sightseeing tour 観光ツアー kankoo tsuaa

sign v 署名します／サインします shomeeshimasu/ sainshimasu

silk 絹 kinu

silver 銀 gin

single (unmarried) 独身 dokushin

single bed シングルベッド shinguru beddo

single room シングルルーム shinguru ruumu

sink 流し nagashi

sister (my older) 姉 ane

sister (my younger) 妹 imooto

sister (someone else's older) お姉さん oneesan

sister (someone else's younger) 妹さん imootosan

sit v 座ります suwarimasu

size サイズ saizu

skin 皮膚 hifu

skirt スカート sukaato

ski スキー sukii

ski lift スキーリフト sukii rifuto

sleep v 眠ります nemurimasu

sleeper car 寝台車 shindaisha

sleeping bag 寝袋／スリーピングバッグ nebukuro/suriipingu baggu

slice (of something) 一切れ hitokire

slippers スリッパ surippa

slower もっとゆっくり motto yukkuri

slowly ゆっくり yukkuri

small 小さい chiisai

smaller もっと小さい motto chiisai

smoke v 煙草を吸います tabako o suimasu

smoking (area) 喫煙席 kitsuenseki

snack bar スナックバー sunakku baa

sneaker スニーカー suniikaa

snorkeling equipment スノーケル用具 sunookeru yoogu

snowboard スノーボード sunoo boodo

snowshoe 雪靴 yukigutsu

snowy 雪の多い yuki no ooi

soap 石鹸 sekken

soccer サッカー sakkaa

sock 靴下 kutsushita

soother [BE] おしゃぶり oshaburi

sore throat 喉の痛み nodo no itami

sorry ごめんなさい gomennasai

south 南 minami

souvenir お土産 omiyage

souvenir store お土産屋 omiyageya

spa 温泉 onsen

spatula へら hera

speak v 話します hanashimasu

specialist (doctor) 専門医 senmon-i

specimen 見本 mihon

speeding スピード違反 supiido ihan

spell v つづりを言います tsuzuri o iimasu

spicy 辛い karai

spine (body part) 脊椎 sekitsui

spoon スプーン supuun

sports スポーツ supootsu

sporting goods store スポーツ用品店 supootsu yoohinten

sprain 捻挫 nenza

stadium スタジアム sutajiamu

stairs 階段 kaidan

stamp n (postage) 切手 kitte

start v (a car) スタートします sutaato shimasu

starter [BE] 前菜 zensai

station 駅 eki

statue 銅像 doozoo

stay v 泊まります tomarimasu

steal v 盗みます nusumimasu

steep 急斜面 kyuushamen

sterling silver 純銀 jungin

sting n 虫さされ mushi sasare

stolen 盗まれた nusumareta

stomach 胃 i

stomachache 腹痛 fukutsuu

stop v 止まります tomarimasu; ~ (bus) n バス停 basu tee

store directory 店内の案内 tennai no annai

storey [BE] 階 kai

stove コンロ konro

straight 真っ直ぐ massugu

strange 変 hen

stream 小川 ogawa

...Street ...通り ...doori

stroller ベビーカー bebiikaa

student 学生 gakusee

study v 勉強します benkyoo shimasu

stunning 驚くほどの odoroku hodono

subtitle (movie) 字幕 jimaku

subway 地下鉄 chikatetsu

subway station 地下鉄の駅 chikatetsu no eki

suit スーツ suutsu

suitcase スーツケース suutsu keesu

sun 太陽 taiyoo

sunblock 日焼け止めクリーム hiyakedome kuriimu

sunburn 日焼け hiyake

sunglasses サングラス sangurasu

sunny 晴れの hareno

sunscreen 日除け hiyoke

sunstroke 日射病 nisshabyoo

super (fuel) スーパー suupaa

supermarket スーパー suupaa

surfboard サーフボード saafu boodo

sushi restaurant 寿司屋 sushi ya

swallow v 呑み込みます nomikomimasu

sweater セーター seetaa

sweatshirt トレーナー toreenaa

sweet (taste) 甘い amai

sweets [BE] キャンデー kyandee

swelling 腫れ hare

swim v 泳ぎます oyogimasu

swimsuit 水着 mizugi

symbol (keyboard) 記号 kigoo

synagogue ユダヤ教会 yudaya kyookai

T

table テーブル teeburu

tablet (medicine) 錠 joo

take v **(medicine)** 飲みます nomimasu

take away [BE] テークアウト teeku auto

tampon タンポン tanpon

taste v 味がします aji ga shimasu

taxi タクシー takushii

tea お茶 ocha

team チーム chiimu

teahouse 喫茶店 kissaten

teaspoon 茶匙 chasaji

telephone 電話 denwa

temple (religious) お寺 otera; ~ **accommodation** 宿坊 shukuboo

temporary 一時的 ichijiteki

tennis テニス tenisu

tent テント tento

tent peg テント用ペグ tento yoo pegu

tent pole テントの支柱 tento no shichuu

terminal (airport) ターミナル taaminaru

terracotta テラコッタ terakotta

terrible ひどい hidoi

text v **(send a message)** メールを送ります meeru o okurimasu; ~ n **(message)** メール meeru

thank v 感謝します kansha shimasu

thank you ありがとう arigatoo

thank you (for food) ごちそうさまでした gochisoo sama deshita

that あれ are

theater 劇場 gekijoo

theft 盗難 toonan

there そこ soko

thief 泥棒 doroboo

thigh 腿 momo

thirsty 喉が渇きました nodo ga kawaki mashita

this これ kore

throat 喉 nodo

ticket 切符 kippu

ticket office 切符売り場 kippu uriba

tie (clothing) ネクタイ nekutai

time 時間 jikan

timetable [BE] 時刻表 jikokuhyoo

tire タイヤ taiya

tired 疲れました tsukare mashita

tissue ティッシュペーパー tisshu peepaa

tobacconist 煙草屋 tabakoya

today 今日 kyoo

toe 足指 ashi yubi

toenail 足の爪 ashi no tsume

toilet [BE] 化粧室 keshooshitsu

toilet paper トイレットペーパー toiretto peepaa

tomorrow あした ashita

tongue 舌 shita

tonight 今晩 konban

too ...過ぎます ...sugimasu

tooth 歯 ha

toothpaste 歯磨き粉 hamigakiko

total (amount) 合計 gookee

tough (food) 硬い katai

tourist 観光客 kankookyaku

tourist information office 観光案内所 kankoo annaijo

tour ツアー tsuaa

tow truck レッカー車 rekkaasha

towel タオル taoru

tower 塔 too

town 町 machi

town hall 市役所 shiyakusho

town map 市街地図 shigai chizu

town square 町の広場 machi no hiroba

toy 玩具 omocha

toy store 玩具屋 omochaya

track (train) 路線 rosen

traditional 伝統的 dentooteki

traffic light 信号 shingoo

trail 道 michi

trail map ハイキングコース案内 haikingu koosu annai

train 列車 ressha; (commuter train) 電車 densha

train station 駅 eki

transfer v (change trains/flights) 乗り換えます norikae masu; ~ v (money) 送金します sookin shimasu

translate v 翻訳します honyaku shimasu

trash ゴミ gomi

travel agency 旅行代理店 ryokoo dairiten

travel sickness 乗物酔い norimono yoi

traveler's check トラベラーズチェック toraberaazu chekku

traveller's cheque [BE] トラベラーズチェック toraberaazu chekku

tree 木 ki

trim v (hair) そろえます soroemasu

trip 旅行 ryokoo

trolley [BE] カート kaato

trousers [BE] ズボン zubon

T-shirt Tシャツ tii shatsu

turn off (lights) 消します keshimasu

turn on (lights) つけます tsukemasu

TV テレビ terebi

type v タイプします taipu shimasu

tyre [BE] タイヤ taiya

U

United Kingdom (U.K.) イギリス igirisu

United States (U.S.) アメリカ amerika

ugly みにくい minikui

umbrella 傘 kasa

unattended 無人の mujinno

unconscious 意識不明の ishiki fumeeno

underground [BE] 地下鉄 chikatetsu

underground station [BE] 地下鉄の駅 chikatetsu no eki

underpants [BE] パンツ pantsu

understand v 分かります wakari masu

underwear 下着 shitagi

university 大学 daigaku

unleaded (gas) 無鉛 muen

upper 上の ueno

urgent 緊急 kinkyuu

use v 使います / 利用します tsukai masu/riyoo shimasu

username ユーザー名 yuuzaa mee

utensil 器具 kigu

V

vacancy 空き室 akishitsu

vacation 休暇 kyuuka

vaccination 予防接種 yoboo sesshu

vacuum cleaner 電気掃除機 denki soojiki

vagina 膣 chitsu

vaginal infection 膣炎 chitsuen

valid 有効 yuukoo

valley 谷間 tanima

valuable 貴重な kichoona

value 値段 nedan

vegetarian ベジタリアン bejitarian

vehicle registration 自動車登録証 jidoosha toorokushoo

viewpoint [BE] 展望台 tenboodai

village 村 mura

vineyard ぶどう園 budooen

visa ビザ biza

visit v 訪れます otozure masu

visiting hours 開館時間 kaikan jikan

visually impaired 視覚障害者 shikaku shoogaisha

vitamin ビタミン bitamin

V-neck ブイネック bui nekku

volleyball game バレーボール試合 bareebooru shiai

vomit v 吐きます hakimasu

W

wait v 待ちます machimasu; ~ n 待ち時間 machi jikan

waiter ウェーター ueetaa

waiting room 待合室 machiaishitsu

waitress ウェートレス ueetoresu

wake v 起こします okoshi masu

wake-up call モーニングコール mooningu kooru

walk v 歩きます aruki masu; ~ n 散歩 sanpo

walking route 散歩道 sanpomichi

wall clock 柱時計 hashira dokee

wallet 財布 saifu

warm v (something) 暖めます atatame masu; ~ adj (temperature) 暖かい atatakai

washing machine 洗濯機 sentakuki

watch 腕時計 ude dokee

water 水 mizu

water skis 水上スキー suijoo sukii

waterfall 滝 taki

weather 天気 tenki

week 週 shuu

weekend 週末 shuumatsu

weekly 毎週 maishuu

welcome v 歓迎します kangee shimasu

well-rested よく休みました yoku yasumi mashita

west 西 nishi

what 何 nani

wheelchair 車椅子 kuruma isu

wheelchair ramp 車椅子用スロープ kuruma isu yoo suroopu

when いつ itsu

where どこ doko

white 白い shiroi

who 誰 dare

widowed 夫と死別した otto to shibetsu shita

wife (one's own) 家内 kanai; (someone else's) 奥さん okusan

window 窓 mado; ~ (on flight) 窓側 madogawa; by the ~ 窓際 madogiwa

wine list ワインリスト wain risuto

winter 冬 fuyu

wireless internet ワイアレスインターネット waiaresu intaanetto

wireless internet service ワイアレスインターネット サービス waiaresu intaanetto saabisu

wireless phone 携帯電話 keetai denwa

with (attached) …付き tsuki; (included) …込み komi

withdraw v 引き出します hikidashi masu

withdrawal (bank) 引き出し hikidashi

without 無しで nashide

woman 女性 josee

wool ウール uuru
work v 働きます hataraki masu
wrap v **(a package)** 包みます
　tsutsumi masu
wrist 手首 tekubi
write v 書きます kaki masu

Y

year 年 toshi
yellow 黄色 kiiro
yen 円 en

yes はい hai
yesterday 昨日 kinoo
young 若い wakai
you're welcome どういたしまし
　て doo itashi mashite
youth hostel ユースホステル
　yuusu hosuteru

Z

zero ゼロ / 零 zero/ree
zoo 動物園 doobutsuen

JAPANESE-ENGLISH

A

aakeedo アーケード arcade

abunai 危ない dangerous

adaputa アダプタ adapter

afutaa sheebu アフターシェーブ aftershave

agemasu あげます *v* give

ago 顎 jaw

ai 愛 love

aida 間 during

aimasu 合います fit (clothing)

airon アイロン iron

airon o kakemasu アイロンをかけます *v* iron (clothing)

airurando アイルランド Ireland

airurando jin アイルランド人 Irish

aisu hokkee アイスホッケー ice hockey

aiteimasu 空いています free (available)

aiteiru 開いている *adj* open

aji ga shimasu 味がします *v* taste

aji ga usui 味が薄い bland

ajia no アジアの Asian

akai 赤い red

akachan 赤ちゃん baby

akari 明かり light (overhead)

akemasu 開けます *v* open

akishitsu 空き室 vacancy

akusesarii アクセサリー accessories

akusesu shimasu アクセスします *v* access (Internet)

amai 甘い sweet (taste)

ame 雨 rain

ameno 雨の rainy

amerika no アメリカの American

amerika アメリカ United States (U.S.)

ane 姉 sister (my older)

ani 兄 brother (my older)

annai 案内 information (phone)

anshoo bangoo 暗証番号 personal identification number (PIN)

anzen 安全 safe (protected)

are あれ that

arerugii hannoo アレルギー反応 allergic reaction

arerugii アレルギー allergic

arigatoo ありがとう thank you

arimasu あります *v* have

aroma serapii アロマセラピー aromatherapy

aruki masu 歩きます *v* walk

arumi hoiru アルミホイル aluminum foil

asa 朝 morning

asa 麻 linen

asetaminoofen アセタミノーフェン paracetamol *[BE]*

ashi no tsume 足の爪 toenail

ashi 脚 leg

ashi 足 foot

ashikubi 足首 ankle

ashita あした tomorrow

atama 頭 head (body part)

atarashii 新しい fresh

atatakai 暖かい *adj* warm (temperature)

atatame masu 暖めます *v* warm (something)

ato 後 after

atode あとで later

atorakushon アトラクション attraction (place)

atsui 暑い hot (temperature)

azukemasu 預けます *v* deposit (money); check (luggage)

B

baa バー bar (place)

baggu バッグ bag

baiten 売店 gift shop

bakkin 罰金 fine (fee)

baree バレエ ballet

bareebooru no shiai バレーボールの試合 volleyball game

baria furii setsubi バリアフリー設備 disabled accessible *[BE]*

basho 場所 *n* place

basu バス bus

basu no kippu バスの切符 bus ticket

basu ryokoo バス旅行 bus tour

basu taaminaru バスターミナル bus station

basu teeryuujo バス停留所 bus stop

basuketto booru バスケットボール basketball

basutee バス停 bus stop

bebii beddo ベビーベッド crib

bebii kaa ベビーカー pushchair *[BE]*

bebii saakuru ベビーサークル playpen

bebii shittaa ベビーシッター babysitter

beddo ベッド bed

beeju ベージュ beige

bejitarian ベジタリアン vegetarian

bekkyo 別居 separated (marriage)

bengoshi 弁護士 lawyer

benjo 便所 restroom (informal)/toilet *[BE]* (informal)

benkyoo shimasu 勉強します *v* study

benpi 便秘 constipated

beruto ベルト belt

biichi ビーチ beach

bijinesu kurasu ビジネス・クラス business class

bijinesu sentaa ビジネス・センター business center

bikini ビキニ bikini

bin 便 flight

bin 瓶 jar

biru ビル building

bitamin ビタミン vitamin

biyooin 美容院 hair salon

biza ビザ visa

boku 僕 I (male, informal)

bonyuu o agemasu 母乳をあげます breastfeed

booi furendo ボーイフレンド boyfriend

bookoo 膀胱 bladder

booru ボール bowl

booshi 帽子 hat

booto ボート rowboat

bubun 部分 portion

budooen ぶどう園 vineyard

buhin 部品 part (for car)

bui nekku ブイネック V-neck

burajaa ブラジャー bra

burausu ブラウス blouse

bureeki ブレーキ brakes (car)

buresuretto ブレスレット bracelet

buriifu ブリーフ briefs

buroochi ブローチ brooch

buruu ブルー blue

butsukarimasu ぶつかります v crash (car)

buutsu ブーツ boots

byooin 病院 hospital

byooki 病気 sick

C

chairo 茶色 brown

chairudo shiito チャイルドシート car seat

chasaji 茶匙 teaspoon

chekku チェック check

chekku auto チェックアウト check-out (hotel)

chekku in チェックイン check-in

chibusa 乳房 breast

chichi 父 father (one's own)

chihoo 地方 local

chiiki 地域 region

chiimu チーム team

chiisai 小さい small

chikai 近い close

chikaku 近く nearby

chikatetsu 地下鉄 subway/underground [BE]

chikatetsu no eki 地下鉄の駅 subway station/underground [BE] station

chitsu 膣 vagina

chitsuen 膣炎 vaginal infection

chizu 地図 n map

choo 腸 intestine

choogoo shimasu 調合します v fill/make up [BE] (a prescription)

chooka 超過 excess

chooshoku 朝食 breakfast

chotto ちょっと little

chuugurai 中ぐらい medium (size)

chuumon shimasu 注文します v order

chuusee senzai 中性洗剤 dishwashing liquid

chuusha shimasu 駐車します v park

chuushajoo 駐車場 parking garage/car park [BE]

chuushoku 昼食 lunch

D

daasu ダース dozen

daburu beddo ダブルベッド double bed

daiamondo ダイアモンド diamond

daidokoro 台所 kitchen

daigaku 大学 university

dainingu ruumu ダイニングルーム dining room

dairiten 代理店 agency

daiseedoo 大聖堂 cathedral

danboo 暖房 heater/heating [BE]

dansu kurabu ダンスクラブ dance club

dare 誰 who

debitto kaado デビットカード debit card

deguchi 出口 exit

dejitaru デジタル digital

dejitaru kamera デジタルカメラ digital camera

dejitaru kamera purinto デジタルカメラプリント digital print

dejitaru shashin デジタル写真 digital photo

dekki chea デッキチェア deck chair

demasu 出ます v leave

denchi 電池 battery

denimu デニム denim

denki soojiki 電気掃除機 vacuum cleaner

denkyuu 電球 lightbulb

densensee 伝染性 contagious

densha 電車 train (commuter)

denshi meeru 電子メール e-mail

denshi meeru adoresu 電子メールアドレス e-mail address

denshi renji 電子レンジ microwave

dentoo 電灯 light (overhead)

dentooteki 伝統的 traditional

denwa 電話 telephone

denwa bangoo 電話番号 phone number

denwa o kakemasu 電話をかけます v dial

denwa shimasu 電話します v phone

deodoranto デオドラント deodorant

depaato デパート department store

derikatessen デリカテッセン delicatessen

dii bui dii DVD DVD

diizeru ディーゼル diesel

do 度 degrees (temperature)

dochira どちら which (polite)

doki 土器 clay pot

doko どこ where

doku 毒 poison

dokushin 独身 single (unmarried)

dono kurai どのくらい how much (quantity)

doo 銅 copper

doo itashi mashite どういたしまして you're welcome

doobutsu 動物 animal

doobutsuen 動物園 zoo

doogu 道具 equipment

dookutsu 洞窟 cave

doomo どうも hi

doomyaku 動脈 artery

…doori …通り …Street

dooro 道路 path

dooro chizu 道路地図 road map

dooryoo 同僚 colleague

dooyatte どうやって how

doozo どうぞ go ahead; please

doozoo 銅像 statue

dorai kuriiningu ten ドライクリーニング店 dry cleaner

dorinku menyuu ドリンクメニュー drink menu

doroboo 泥棒 thief

doru ドル dollar (U.S.)

dotchi どっち which

E

eakon エアコン air conditioning

eaponpu エアポンプ air pump

eega 映画 movie

eegakan 映画館 movie theater

eego 英語 English (language)

eegyoo jikan 営業時間 business hours

eekokujin 英国人 British

eetiiemu キャッシュコーナー ATM

eezu エイズ AIDS

eki 駅 train station/railway station [BE]

ekonomii kurasu エコノミークラス economy class

ekusukaashon エクスカーション excursion

en 円 yen

enshi 遠視 far-sighted/long-sighted [BE]

erebeetaa エレベーター elevator/lift [BE]

esukareetaa エスカレーター escalator

F

faasuto fuudo ファーストフード fast food

faasuto kurasu ファーストクラス first class

fakkusu ファックス fax

fakkusu bangoo ファックス番号 fax number

fakkusu shimasu ファックスします v fax

feesharu フェーシャル facial

ferii フェリー ferry

fiirudo フィールド field (sports)

fooku フォーク fork

fooku myuujikku フォークミュージック folk music

fuirumu フィルム film (camera)

fujinkai 婦人科医 gynecologist

fukaku 深く deeply

fukanabe 深鍋 pot

fukumimasu 含みます v include

fukusayoo 副作用 side effect

fukusoo kitee 服装規定 dress code

fukutsuu 腹痛 stomachache

fuminshoo 不眠症 insomnia

fun 分 minute

funsui 噴水 fountain

furaipan フライパン frying pan

furoba 風呂場 bathroom

furui 古い old (thing)

futsuka yoi 二日酔い hangover

futsuu yokin 普通預金 savings (account)

fuutoo 封筒 envelope

fuyu 冬 winter

G

gaaru furendo ガールフレンド girlfriend

gaido ガイド n guide

gaido bukku ガイドブック guide book

gaikokujin 外国人 foreigner

gake 崖 cliff

gakkiya 楽器屋 music store

gakkoo 学校 school

gakusee 学生 student

gamu ガム chewing gum

garasu ガラス glass (material)

gasorin ガソリン gas/petrol [BE]

gasorin sutando ガソリンスタンド gas station/petrol station [BE]

gasu ガス cooking gas

geemu ゲーム game

geeto ゲート gate (airport)

gei baa ゲイバー gay bar

gei kurabu ゲイクラブ gay club

gekijoo 劇場 theater

genkin 現金 cash

gerende ゲレンデ trail/piste [BE]

gerende chizu ゲレンデ地図 trail/piste [BE] map

geri 下痢 diarrhea

gifuto shoppu ギフトショップ gift shop

gin 銀 silver

ginkoo 銀行 bank

gochisoo sama deshita ごちそうさまでした thank you (for food)

godengon ご伝言 message

gogo 午後 afternoon/p.m.

gomen kudasai ごめんください bye

gomennasai ごめんなさい sorry

gomi ゴミ trash/rubbish [BE]

gomi bukuro ゴミ袋 garbage bag/rubbish bag [BE]

gookan 強姦 rape

gookee 合計 total (amount)

gorufu toonamento ゴルフトーナメント golf tournament

gorufujoo ゴルフ場 golf course

goshujin ご主人 husband (someone else's)

gozen 午前 a.m.

guramu グラム gram

gurasu グラス glass (drinking)

guree グレー gray

guriin グリーン green

guruupu グループ group

H

ha 歯 tooth

hagaki 葉書 postcard

haha 母 mother (one's own)

hai はい yes

hai 肺 lung

haicheaa ハイチェアー highchair

haiiro 灰色 gray

haikingu koosu annai ハイキングコース案内 trail/piste [BE] map

hairimasu 入ります v enter

haisha 歯医者 dentist

haiuee ハイウェー highway

hajime masu 始めます v begin

hakarimasu 測ります v measure (someone)

hakike 吐き気 nauseous

hakimasu 吐きます v vomit

hako 箱 box

hakubutsukan 博物館 museum

hamaki 葉巻 cigar

hamigakiko 歯磨き粉 toothpaste

han jikan 半時間 half hour

han kiro 半キロ half-kilo

hana 花 flower

hana 鼻 nose

hanashimasu 話します v speak

hanbun 半分 half

handi kyappuyoo ハンディキャップ用 handicapped-accessible

hando baggu ハンドバッグ purse/handbag [BE]

hankagai 繁華街 downtown

hanmaa ハンマー hammer

hansode 半袖 short sleeves

hanzubon 半ズボン shorts

haraimasu 払います v pay

hare 腫れ swelling

hareno 晴れの sunny

hari 鍼 acupuncture

hasami はさみ scissors

hashi 橋 bridge

hashira dokee 柱時計 wall clock

hasshin 発疹 rash

hatarakimasu 働きます v work

hatsuon shimasu 発音します v pronounce

hayai 早い early

hayai 速い fast

hea burashi ヘアブラシ hairbrush

hea doraiyaa ヘアドライヤー hair dryer

hea katto ヘアカット haircut

hea supuree ヘアスプレー hairspray

hea sutairisuto ヘアスタイリスト hairstylist

hea sutairu ヘアスタイル hairstyle

heddofoon ヘッドフォーン headphones

heekan 閉館 closed

heeten 閉店 closed

hen 変 strange

henkoo 変更 change (plan)

hera へら spatula

herumetto ヘルメット helmet

heya 部屋 room

heya no kagi 部屋の鍵 room key

hi o tsukemasu 火をつけます v light (cigarette)

hi 日 day

hi 火 fire

hidari 左 left (direction)

hifu 皮膚 skin

higashi 東 east

hiitaa ヒーター heater/heating [BE]

hiji 肘 elbow

hijoo guchi 非常口 emergency exit

hikidashi 引き出し withdrawal (bank)

hikidashi masu 引き出します v withdraw

hikkimasu 引きます v pull

hikooki 飛行機 airplane

hikui 低い low

hima 暇 free (not busy)

hinketsu no 貧血の anemic

hiruma 昼間 noon/midday [BE]

hitchi haiku shimasu ヒッチハイクします v hitchhike

hitoban ni tsuki 一晩につき per night

hitokire 一切れ slice (of something)

hitori 一人 alone

hitotsu 一つ one

hiyake 日焼け sunburn

hiyakedome kuriimu 日焼け止めクリーム sunblock

hiyoke 日除け sunscreen

hiyoo 費用 fee

hiza 膝 knee

hizuke 日付け date (calendar)

hoka no michi 他の道 alternate route

hoken 保険 insurance

hoken gaisha 保険会社 insurance company

hoken o kakemasu 保険を掛けます v insure

hokenshoo 保険証 insurance card

hokkee ホッケー hockey

hokoosha 歩行者 pedestrian

hon 本 book

hone 骨 bone

honmono 本物 real

hon-ya 本屋 bookstore

hon-yaku shimasu 翻訳します v translate

honyuubin 哺乳瓶 baby bottle

hooki 箒 broom

hookoo 方向 direction

hoomu ホーム platform

hooseki 宝石 jewelry

hoosekiten 宝石店 jeweler

hootai 包帯 bandage

horikomimasu 彫り込みます v engrave

hoshiin desuga 欲しいんですが I'd like…

hosuteru ホステル hostel

hoteru ホテル hotel

hozon shimasu 保存します v save (on a computer)

hyooji 表示 display

I

i 胃 stomach

ibupurofen イブプロフェン ibuprofen

ichiban ii 一番いい best

ichido 一度 once

ichiinichiikan 一日間 for (a day)

ichijikan ni tsuki 一時間につき per hour

ichijiteki 一時的 temporary

ichinichi ni tsuki 一日につき per day

idoosee 移動性 mobility

ie 家 house

igirisu イギリス United Kingdom (U.K.)

igirisujin イギリス人 English

ii 良い good

iichiketto Eチケット e-ticket

iie いいえ no

ike 池 pond

iki 行き bound

iki masu 行きます v go

ikkai 一階 ground floor

ikura いくら how much (money)

ima 今 now

imooto 妹 sister (my younger)

imootosan 妹さん sister (someone else's younger)

inakunaru いなくなる missing
inryoosui 飲料水 drinking water
insatsu shimasu 印刷します v print
insurin インスリン insulin
insutanto messeeji インスタント・メッセージ instant message
intaanetto インターネット internet
intaanetto kafe インターネットカフェ internet cafe
intaanetto saabisu インターネットサービス internet service
ippoo tsuukoo 一方通行 one-way street
ireba 入れ歯 denture
iremasu 入れます v insert (on an ATM)
iriguchi 入口 entrance
irimasu 要ります v need
iro 色 color
irui 衣類 clothing
iseki 遺跡 ruins
isha 医者 doctor
ishiki fumeino 意識不明の unconscious
ishitsubutu gakari 遺失物係 lost and found
issho 一緒 together
isshuukan ni tsuki 一週間につき per week
isu 椅子 chair
itai 痛い hurt

itami 痛み pain
itsu いつ when
itteki 一滴 drop (medicine)
iyaringu イヤリング earrings

J

jaketto ジャケット jacket
jazu ジャズ jazz
jazu kurabu ジャズクラブ jazz club
jeru ジェル gel (hair)
jidoo 自動 automatic
jidoosha toorokushoo 自動車登録証 vehicle registration
jiinzu ジーンズ jeans
jikan 時間 hour/time
jiko 事故 accident
jikokuhyoo 時刻表 timetable [BE]
jimaku 字幕 subtitle (movie)
jinja 神社 shrine
jinzoo 腎臓 kidney (body part)
jitensha 自転車 bicycle
jitensha ruuto 自転車ルート bike route
joo 錠 tablet (medicine)
jookyaku 乗客 passenger
joosha shimasu 乗車します v board (train)
josee 女性 woman
jungin 純銀 sterling silver
junyuu shimasu 授乳します v feed (baby)
juuden shimasu 充電します v recharge

juusho 住所 address

K

kaado カード card

kaado de haraimasu カードで払います v charge (credit card)

kaato カート cart/trolley [BE]

kaaton カートン carton

kabaa chaaji カバーチャージ cover charge

kado no 角の on the corner

kado o magatta tokoro 角を曲がったところ around (the corner)

kaemasu 替えます v exchange (money)

kaeshimasu 返します v return

kagaku 科学 science

kagi 鍵 key; lock

kagi o kakemasu 鍵をかけます lock up

kago かご basket (grocery store)

kai 階 floor/storey [BE]

kaichuu dentoo 懐中電灯 flashlight

kaidan 階段 stairs

kaigan 海岸 beach

kaigi 会議 meeting

kaigijoo 会議場 convention hall

kaigishitsu 会議室 meeting room

kaiin shoo 会員証 membership card

kaikan jikan 開館時間 visiting hours

kaikee 会計 n bill (of sale); cashier

kaikyoo jiin 回教寺院 mosque

kaimasu 買います v buy

kaimono 買い物 shopping

kaimono o shimasu 買い物をします v shop

kajino カジノ casino

kakarimasu かかります v cost

kakekin o haraimasu 掛け金を払います v place (a bet)

kaki masu 書きます v write

kakitome 書留 registered mail

kakunin shimasu 確認します v confirm

kamera カメラ camera

kami 紙 paper

kami 髪 hair

kamisori no ha カミソリの刃 razor blade

kanada カナダ Canada

kanadajin カナダ人 Canadian

kanai 家内 wife (one's own)

kanashii 悲しい sad

kangei shimasu 歓迎します v welcome

kangoshi 看護士 nurse

kankee 関係 relationship

kankin shimasu 換金します v exchange (money)

kankiri 缶切り can opener

kankoo 観光 sightseeing
kankoo annaijo 観光案内所 tourist information office
kankoo tsuaa 観光ツアー sightseeing tour
kankookyaku 観光客 tourist
kansen shita 感染した infected
kansetsu 関節 joint (body part)
kansetsuen 関節炎 arthritis
kansha shimasu 感謝します v thank
kanyuu shimasu 加入します v join
kanzee 関税 duty (tax)
kanzen saabisu 完全サービス full-service
kanzoo 肝臓 liver (body part)
kanzume 缶詰 canned
kao 顔 face
kappu カップ cup
kara ni shimasu 空にします v empty
karafu カラフ carafe
karai 辛い hot (spicy)
karimasu 借ります v rent
karorii カロリー calories
kasa 傘 umbrella
kata 肩 shoulder
katai 硬い tough (food)
katamichi 片道 one-way (ticket)
katee yoohin 家庭用品 household good
katto カット v cut (hair)

kawa 川 river
kawa 皮 leather
kawaii 可愛い cute
kawasereeto 為替レート exchange rate
kaze 風邪 cold (sickness)
kazoku 家族 family
keebajoo 競馬場 racetrack
keebi 警備 security
keeburu kaa ケーブル・カー cable car
keekiya ケーキ屋 pastry shop
keeryoo kappu 計量カップ measuring cup
keeryoo supuun 計量スプーン measuring spoon
keesatsu 警察 police
keesatsu no shoomeesho 警察の証明書 police report
keesu ケース case (amount)
keetai denwa 携帯電話 cell phone/mobile phone [BE]
kekkon shimasu 結婚します v marry
kekkon shiteiru 結婚している married
kemikaru toire ケミカルトイレ chemical toilet
kenkoo 健康 health
kenkoo shokuhinten 健康食品店 health food store
keshi masu 消します turn off (lights)
keshooshitsu 化粧室 restroom/toilet [BE]

ketsuatsu 血圧 blood pressure

ketsueki 血液 blood

ki 木 tree

kichoona 貴重な valuable

kigoo 記号 symbol (keyboard)

kigu 器具 utensil

kii horudaa キーホルダー key ring

kii kaado キーカード

kiiro 黄色 yellow

kikan 期間 period (of time)

kimasu 来ます v come

kin 金 gold

kin-en 禁煙 non-smoking

kinenkan 記念館 memorial (place)

kinko 金庫 safe (thing)

kinkyuu 緊急 emergent

kinniku 筋肉 muscle

kinoo 昨日 yesterday

kinshi shimasu 禁止します v prohibit

kinshi 近視 near-sighted/ short-sighted [BE]

kinu 絹 silk

kinyuu shimasu 記入します v fill out (form)

kinyuu shite kudasai 記入して ください please fill out (form)

kiosuku キオスク newsstand

kippu 切符 ticket

kippu uriba 切符売り場 ticket office

kiree きれい clean; beautiful

kiro(guramu) キロ(グラム) kilogram

kiro(meetoru) キロ(メートル) kilometer

kissaten 喫茶店 café/ teahouse

kisu shimasu キスします v kiss

kita 北 north

kitanai 汚い dirty

kitsuenseki 喫煙席 smoking (area)

kitte 切手 n stamp (postage)

kizu 傷 n cut

kizugusuri 傷薬 antiseptic cream

kodomo 子供 child

kodomoyoo no isu 子供用の 椅子 child's seat

kodomoyoo no menyuu 子 供用のメニュー children's menu

kodomoyoo puuru 子供用プ ール kiddie pool/paddling pool [BE]

koin randorii コインランドリー laundromat/launderette [BE]

koin rokkaa コインロッカー luggage locker

koko ここ here

kokunai no 国内の domestic

kokunaisen 国内線 domestic flight

kokusai 国際 international (airport area)

kokusaisen 国際線 international flight

kokuseki 国籍 nationality

kokyuu shimasu 呼吸します v breathe

...komi ...込み with ... (included)

konban 今晩 tonight

konbanwa 今晩は good evening

konbeyaa beruto コンベヤーベルト conveyor belt

kondishonaa コンディショナー conditioner

kondoomu コンドーム condom

konnichiwa こんにちは hello; good afternoon

konpyuuta コンピュータ computer

konro コンロ stove

konsaato コンサート concert

konsaato hooru コンサートホール concert hall

konsarutanto コンサルタント consultant

konsento コンセント electric outlet

kontakuto renzu コンタクトレンズ contact lens

kontakuto renzu eki コンタクトレンズ液 contact lens solution

konzatsu 混雑 congestion

kooban 交番 police station

karai 辛い spicy

kooen 公園 n park/playground

kooka 硬貨 coin

kookanjo 交換所 exchange (place)

kookuu gaisha 航空会社 airline

kookuubin 航空便 airmail

kookyoo 公共 public

kooreesha 高齢者 senior citizen

koori 氷 ice

kooryoku fuyoo 抗力浮揚 drag lift

koosaten 交差点 intersection

koosee busshitsu 抗生物質 antibiotic

koosha コーシャ kosher

kooshuu denwa 公衆電話 pay phone

koosoku dooro 高速道路 highway/motorway [BE]

koosu コース route

koosui 香水 perfume

kooto コート coat

kopii コピー photocopy

koppu コップ glass (drinking)

kore これ this

koruku sukuryuu コルクスクリュー corkscrew

koshoo 故障 breakdown

kotton コットン cotton

kottooten 骨董店 antiques store

kowaremasu 壊れます v damage

kowareta 壊れた damaged

kozutsumi 小包 package

kubi 首 neck

kuchi 口 mouth

kuchibiru 唇 lip

kujoo 苦情 complaint

kuni bangoo 国番号 country code

kurabu クラブ club

kurai 暗い dark

kurashikku ongaku クラシック音楽 classical music

kurasu クラス class

kurejitto kaado クレジットカード credit card

kuriiningu yoohin クリーニング用品 cleaning supplies

kuroi 黒い black

kuruma 車 car

kuruma isu 車椅子 wheelchair

kuruma isu yoo suroopu 車椅子用スロープ wheelchair ramp

kuruu nekku クルーネック crew neck

kushi 櫛 comb

kusuri 薬 medicine

kutsu 靴 shoes

kutsushita 靴下 sock

kutsuya 靴屋 shoe store

kuukoo 空港 airport

kyabin キャビン cabin

kyakushitsu seesoo saabisu 客室清掃サービス housekeeping services

kyandee キャンデー candy/sweets [BE]

kyanpu kinshi キャンプ禁止 no camping

kyanpu shimasu キャンプします v camp

kyanpujoo キャンプ場 campsite

kyanseru shimasu キャンセルします v cancel

kyasshingu saabisu キャッシング・サービス cash advance

kyasshu kaado キャッシュカード ATM card

kyohi shimasu 拒否します v decline (credit card)

kyoka shimasu 許可します v permit

kyoo 今日 today

kyookai 教会 church

kyori 距離 mileage

kyuuden 宮殿 palace

kyuuka 休暇 vacation/holiday [BE]

kyuushamen 急斜面 steep

kyuukyuusha 救急車 ambulance

kyuumee booto 救命ボート life boat

kyuumee dooi 救命胴衣 life jacket

M

maaketto マーケット market

machi 町 town

machi jikan 待ち時間 *n* wait

machi no hiroba 町の広場 town square

machiaishitsu 待合室 waiting room

machiawasemasu 待ち合わせます *v* meet (someone)

machigai 間違い mistake

machimasu 待ちます *v* wait

mado 窓 window

madogawa 窓側 window (on flight)

madogiwa 窓際 by the window

mae 前 before

maekin 前金 deposit (security)

mago 孫 grandchild

maishuu 毎週 weekly

majimena 真面目な serious

makura 枕 pillow

manikyua マニキュア manicure

manshon マンション apartment

mantan ni shimasu 満タンにします *v* fill up (gasoline)

manyuaru マニュアル manual car

massaaji マッサージ massage

massugu 真っ直ぐ straight

masui 麻酔 anesthesia

maunten baiku マウンテンバイク mountain bike

mayonaka 真夜中 midnight

me 目 eye

meeru o okurimasu メールを送ります *v* text (send a message)

meeru shimasu メールします *v* e-mail

meeru メール *n* text (message)

meesaisho 明細書 itemized bill

meeshi 名刺 business card

megane 眼鏡 glasses

meganeten 眼鏡店 optician

memai ga shimasu めまいがします dizzy

memorii kaado メモリーカード memory card

men 綿 cotton

menyuu メニュー menu

menzee 免税 duty-free

messeeji メッセージ message

mibun shoomee 身分証明 identification

michi ni mayoi mashita 道に迷いました lost

michi 道 trail

midori 緑 green

migi 右 right (direction)

miharashidai 見晴し台 overlook (scenic place)

mihon 見本 specimen

mijikai 短い short

mimasu 見ます *v* see

mimasu 見ます *v* look

mimi 耳 ear

mimi ga kikoenai 耳が聞こえない deaf

mimi no itami 耳の痛み earache

minami 南 south

mini baa ミニバー mini-bar

minikui みにくい ugly

miruku ミルク milk (baby)

miryokuteki 魅力的 attractive

misa ミサ mass (church service)

misemasu 見せます v show

mizu 水 water

mizugi 水着 swimsuit

mizuumi 湖 lake

mochikomemasu 持ち込めます v allowed (on flight)

momo 腿 thigh

mondai 問題 problem

moo ichido iimasu もう一度言います v repeat

moochoo 盲腸 appendix (body part)

moodoo ken 盲導犬 guide dog

moofu 毛布 blanket

mooningu kooru モーニングコール wake-up call

mootaa booto モーターボート motor boat

mopetto モペット moped

moppu モップ mop

mori 森 forest

moshi moshi もしもし hello (on the phone)

motto もっと more

motto chiisai もっと小さい smaller

motto ii もっといい better

motto ookii もっと大きい bigger

motto ookii koe de もっと大きい声で louder

motto sukunai もっと少ない less

motto yasui もっと安い cheaper

motto yukkuri もっとゆっくり slower

muen 無鉛 unleaded (gas)

mujinno 無人の unattended

mukai 向かい opposite

mune 胸 chest (body part)

mune no itami 胸の痛み chest pain

mura 村 village

murasaki 紫 purple

muryoo 無料 free

mushi sasare 虫さされ insect bite

mushi yoke 虫除け insect repellent

mushi 虫 bug

mushiboo 無脂肪 fat free

mushiki 蒸し器 steamer

muusu ムース mousse (hair)

muzukashii 難しい difficult

N

nabe 鍋 saucepan

nagai 長い long

nagashi 流し sink

nagasode 長袖 long sleeves

naifu ナイフ knife

naisen 内線 extension (phone)

naito kurabu ナイトクラブ nightclub

nakushimasu なくします v lose (something)

namae 名前 name

nandemo 何でも anything

nani 何 what

nankoo 軟膏 cream (ointment)

naosemasu 直せます can fix (clothing)

naoshi masu 直します v alter (clothing)/fix

napukin ナプキン napkin

nashide 無しで without

nebukuro 寝袋 sleeping bag

nedan 値段 price/value

neeru fairu ネイルファイル nail file

neeru saron ネイルサロン nail salon

nekkuresu ネックレス necklace

nekutai ネクタイ tie (clothing)

nemuke 眠気 drowsiness

nemurimasu 眠ります v sleep

nenree 年齢 age

nenza 捻挫 sprain

netsu 熱 fever; heat

nihongo 日本語 Japanese (language)

nihonjin 日本人 Japanese (people)

nikuya 肉屋 butcher

nimotsu 荷物 luggage/ baggage [BE]

nimotsu hikikae ken 荷物引換券 luggage ticket

nimotsu hikikaeshoo 荷物引換証 baggage ticket

ningyoo 人形 doll

ninshin 妊娠 pregnant

nishi 西 west

nisshabyoo 日射病 sunstroke

nitsuki につき per

no tame ni のために for

nodo 喉 throat

nodo ga kawaki mashita 喉が渇きました thirsty

nodo no itami 喉の痛み sore throat

nomikomimasu 呑み込みます v swallow

nomimasu 飲みます v drink; take (medicine)

nomimono 飲み物 drink

non arukooru ノンアルコール non-alcoholic

nooka 農家 farm

norikae masu 乗り換えます v transfer (train/flight)

norimono yoi 乗り物酔い motion sickness

nugimasu 脱ぎます take off (shoes)

nukimasu 抜きます v extract (tooth)

nusumaremashita 盗まれました robbed

nusumareta 盗まれた stolen

nusumimasu 盗みます v rob

nyuukoku tetsuzuki 入国手続き passport control

nyuuryoku shimasu 入力します v enter (computer)

nyuutoo futaishoo 乳糖不耐症 lactose intolerant

O

obaasan おばあさん grandmother (someone else's)

ocha お茶 tea

odorimasu 踊ります v dance

odoroku hodono 驚くほどの stunning

ofisu オフィス office

ofisu awaa オフィスアワー office hours

ogawa 小川 stream

ohashi おはし chopsticks

ohayoo gozaimasu お早うございます good morning

oiru オイル oil

oishii おいしい delicious

ojiisan おじいさん grandfather (someone else's)

oka 丘 hill

okaasan お母さん mother (some one else's)

okane お金 money

okanjoo お勘定 check (payment)

okoshimasu 起こします v wake

okugai puuru 屋外プール outdoor pool

okuremasu 遅れます v delay

okurimasu 送ります v send (mail)

okurimono 贈り物 gift

okusan 奥さん wife (someone else's)

omise kudasai お見せください v show (me)

omiyage お土産 souvenir

omiyageya お土産屋 souvenir store

omocha 玩具 toy

omochaya 玩具屋 toy store

omoshiroi 面白い interesting

omutsu o kaemasu おむつを替えます v change (baby)

omutsu おむつ diaper/nappy [BE]

onaka ga sukimashita お腹がすきました hungry

oneesan お姉さん sister (someone else's older)

onegai shimasu お願いします please (asking for a favor)

ongaku 音楽 music

onna no ko 女の子 girl

oniisan お兄さん brother (someone else's older)

onsen 温泉 hot spring; spa

oodekoron オーデコロン cologne

oofuku 往復 *n* round-trip/ return [BE]

ookee オーケー OK

ookesutora オーケストラ orchestra

ookii 大きい large

oosutorariajin オーストラリア人 Australian

ootobai オートバイ motorcycle

ootomachikku オートマチック automatic car

opera hausu オペラハウス opera house

opera オペラ opera

ore 俺 I (male, informal)

oremasu 折れます *v* break (tooth)

orenji iro オレンジ色 orange (color)

orimasu 下ります get off (train/bus/subway)

oritatami beddo 折り畳みベッド cot

osatsu お札 bill/note [BE]

oshaburi おしゃぶり pacifier/ soother [BE]

oshiete kudasai 教えてください *v* show (tell me)

oshimasu 押します *v* push

oshiri お尻 buttocks

oshirifuki おしりふき baby wipe

oshiro お城 castle

osoi 遅い late (time)

osoimasu 襲います *v* mug (attack)

osoroshii 恐ろしい terrible

osusume desu お薦めです I recommend…

otera お寺 temple (religious)

otoko no ko 男の子 boy

otoko no hito 男の人 man

otoosan お父さん father (someone else's)

otooto 弟 brother (my younger)

otootosan 弟さん brother (someone else's younger)

otozuremasu 訪れます *v* visit

otsumami おつまみ appetizer

otsuri お釣り change (money)

otto to shibetsu shita 夫と死別した widowed

owarimasu 終わります *v* end

oyogimasu 泳ぎます *v* swim

oyu お湯 hot water

P

paato taimu パートタイム part-time

pajama パジャマ pajamas

pansuto パンスト pantyhose/ tights [BE]

pantii パンティー briefs (clothing)

pantsu パンツ underwear/ underpants [BE]

pan-ya パン屋 bakery

pasu waado パスワード password

pasupooto パスポート passport

pedikyua ペディキュア pedicure

peepaa taoru ペーパータオル paper towel

pen ペン pen

penishirin ペニシリン penicillin

penisu ペニス penis

petiito ペティート petite

pikunikkujoo ピクニック場 picnic area

pinku ピンク pink

piru ピル Pill (birth control)

piza resutoran ピザ・レストラン pizzeria

poketto ポケット pocket

pondo ポンド pound (British sterling)

pondo ポンド pound (weight)

popyuraa ongaku ポピュラー音楽 pop music

pun 分 minute

purachina プラチナ platinum

purasu saizu プラス サイズ plus size

purinto shimasu プリントします v print

puripeedo keetai プリペイド携帯 prepaid phone

puuru プール pool

R

raifu gaado ライフガード lifeguard

raitaa ライター lighter

raketto ラケット racket (sports)

randorii saabisu ランドリーサービス laundry service

rappu ラップ plastic wrap/cling film [BE]

rappu ラップ rap (music)

rasshu ラッシュ rush

ree 零 zero

reenkooto レーンコート raincoat

reesu レース lace

reeto レート exchange rate

reetooko 冷凍庫 freezer

reezooko 冷蔵庫 refrigerator

regyuraa レギュラー regular

rekkaasha レッカー車 tow truck

renraku 連絡 connection (flight)

rentakaa レンタカー rental car/hire car BE]

renzu レンズ lens

reshiito レシート receipt

ressha 列車 train

ressun レッスン lesson

resutoran レストラン restaurant

rifuto リフト lift

rifutoken リフト券 lift pass

rikon shimasu 離婚します v divorce

ringu リング ring

rinsu リンス conditioner

rippa 立派 magnificent

risaikuringu リサイクリング recycling

rittoru リットル liter

riyoo shimasu 利用します v utilize

roguofu shimasu ログオフします log off

roguon shimasu ログオンします log on

rokkaa ロッカー locker

rokkotsu 肋骨 rib (body part)

romanchikku ロマンチック romantic

roofaa ローファー loafers

rooshon ローション lotion

rosen 路線 track (train)

ruumu saabisu ルームサービス room service

ryokan 旅館 inn

ryokoo dairiten 旅行代理店 travel agency

ryokoo 旅行 trip

ryoo 寮 dormitory

ryoogae 両替 currency exchange

ryoogae shimasu 両替します v exchange (money)

ryoogaejo 両替所 currency exchange office

ryoojikan 領事館 consulate

ryookin meetaa 料金メーター parking meter

ryookin 料金 charge (cost)

ryoori shimasu 料理します v cook

ryooshuusho 領収書 receipt

ryukkusakku リュックサック backpack

ryuugakuseeshoo 留学生証 international student card

S

saabisu サービス service (in a restaurant)

saafu boodo サーフボード surfboard

sabaku 砂漠 desert

saifu 財布 purse; wallet

saigo 最後 last

saikuringu サイクリング cycling

sainshimasu サインします v sign

saisho no 最初の first

saizu サイズ size

sakana 魚 fish

sakaya 酒屋 liquor store/off-licence [BE]

sakkaa サッカー soccer

sakkaa geemu サッカーゲーム soccer/football [BE] game

sakujo shimasu 削除します v delete

samui 寒い cold (weather)

sandaru サンダル sandals

sangurasu サングラス sunglasses

sanpo 散歩 n walk

sanpomichi 散歩道 walking route

sanshoo 山頂 peak (of a mountain)

sanso chiryoo 酸素治療 oxygen treatment

sara 皿 plate

sauna サウナ sauna

sayoonara さようなら goodbye

seebyoo 性病 sexually transmitted disease (STD)

seekyuu shimasu 請求します v bill (charge)

seekyuusho 請求書 invoice

seeri 生理 period (menstrual)

seeriyoo napukin 生理用ナプキン sanitary napkin/pad [BE]

seetaa セーター sweater

seiritsuu 生理痛 menstrual cramp

seki 咳 cough

seki 席 seat

sekitsui 脊椎 spine (body part)

sekken 石鹸 soap

seminaa セミナー seminar

sen 線 line (train)

senaka 背中 back (body part)

senchi meetoru センチメートル centimeter

senjooato 戦場跡 battleground

senjoozai 洗浄剤 cleaning product

senmon-i 専門医 specialist (doctor)

senmonka 専門家 expert (skill level)

sennuki 栓抜き bottle opener

senpuuki 扇風機 fan (appliance)

sensui yoogu 潜水用具 diving equipment

sentaku 洗濯 laundry

sentaku shisetsu 洗濯施設 laundry facility

sentakuki 洗濯機 washing machine

senzai 洗剤 detergent

serufu saabisu セルフサービス self-service

sesshi 摂氏 Celsius

setomono 瀬戸物 china

setsuzoku 接続 connection (internet)

setsuzoku o kirimasu 接続を切ります disconnect (computer)

setsuzoku shimasu 接続します v connect (internet)

shanpuu シャンプー shampoo

shashin 写真 photo

shashin satsuee 写真撮影 photography

shatsu シャツ shirt

shawaa シャワー shower

sheebingu kuriimu シェービングクリーム shaving cream

shiai 試合 n match

shibai 芝居 n play (theater)

shichakushitsu 試着室 fitting room

shigai chizu 市街地図 town map

shigai kyokuban 市外局番 area code

shigoto 仕事 business

shihainin 支配人 manager (restaurant, hotel)

shihee 紙幣 n bill (money)/ note [BE]

shii dii CD CD

shiitsu シーツ sheet

shikaku shoogaisha 視覚障害者 visually impaired

shikki 漆器 lacquerware

shimasu します v play

shimemasu 閉めます v close (a shop)

shinbun 新聞 newspaper

shindai 寝台 berth

shindaisha 寝台車 sleeper car

shingoo 信号 traffic light

shinguru beddo シングルベッド single bed

shinguru ruumu シングルルーム single room

shinju 真珠 pearl

shinnyuu shimasu 侵入します break-in (burglary)

shintai shoogaisha 身体障害者 disabled; handicapped

shinzoo 心臓 heart

shinzoobyoo 心臓病 heart condition

shirabemasu 調べます v check (something)

shirasemasu 知らせます v notify

shiroi 白い white

shisnkoku shimasu 申告します v declare

shita 舌 tongue

shitagi 下着 underwear

shitsu 質 quality

shitsumon 質問 question

shitsunai puuru 室内プール indoor pool

shitsuree shimasu 失礼します excuse me (to get past)

shiyakusho 市役所 town hall

shizen hogoku 自然保護区 nature preserve

shizuka 静か quiet

shohoo shimasu 処方します v prescribe

shohoosen 処方箋 prescription

shohoosen nashi 処方箋無し over the counter (medication)

shokki 食器 dish (kitchen)

shokubutsuen 植物園 botanical garden

shokudoo 食堂 dining room

shokuji 食事 meal

shokuryoohin 食料品 produce

shokuryoohinten 食料品店 grocery store

shokusen ki 食洗機 dishwasher

shomeeshimasu 署名します
v sign

shooboosho 消防署 fire
department

shoogo 正午 noon

shoohizee 消費税 sales tax

shoojoo 症状 condition
(medical)

shookai shimasu 紹介します *v*
introduce

shookeesu ショーケース
display case

shookyo shimasu 消去します
v clear (on an ATM)

shoonikai 小児科医
pediatrician

shooten gai 商店街 shopping
area

shoppingu mooru ショッピング
モール shopping mall

shoshinsha 初心者 novice
(skill level)

shujin 主人 husband (one's
own)

shukketsu shimasu 出血しま
す *v* bleed

shukuboo 宿坊 temple
accommodation

shukuhaku setsubi 宿泊設備
accommodation

shuppatsu 出発 departure

shusseki shimasu 出席します
v attend

shuu 週 week

shuuji yoogu 習字用具
calligraphy supplies

shuumatsu 週末 weekend

shuuri shimasu 修理します
v repair

shuurikoo 修理工 mechanic

shuurikoojoo 修理工場
garage

sobo 祖母 grandmather (one's
own)

sofu 祖父 grandfather (one's
own)

sofubo 祖父母 grandparents
(one's own)

soko そこ there

sokutatsu 速達 express

sookin shimasu 送金します
v transfer (money)

soonyuu shimasu 挿入します
v insert (on an ATM)

soto 外 outside

...sugimasu …過ぎます too...

sugoi すごい amazing

suihanki 炊飯器 rice cooker

suijoo sukii 水上スキー water
skis

suisen shimasu 推薦します
v recommend

suisen 推薦 recommendation

suishoo 水晶 crystal

sukaafu スカーフ scarf

sukaato スカート skirt

sukidesu 好きです *v* like

sukii スキー ski

sukii rifuto スキーリフト chair lift

sukoshi 少し little

sukyanaa スキャナー scanner

sumi 炭 charcoal

sumimasen すみません excuse me (apology)

sumimasu 住みます v live

sunakku baa スナックバー snack bar

suniikaa スニーカー sneaker

sunoo boodo スノーボード snowboard

sunookeru yoogu スノーケル用具 snorkeling equipment

supiido ihan スピード違反 speeding

supootsu スポーツ sports

supootsu yoohinten スポーツ用品店 sporting goods store

supuun スプーン spoon

suriipingu baggu スリーピングバッグ sleeping bag

surippa スリッパ slippers

surudoi 鋭い sharp

sushi ya 寿司屋 sushi restaurant

sutaato shimasu スタートします v start (a car)

sutajiamu スタジアム stadium

suteki すてき nice

sutokku ストック poles (skiing)

suuji 数字 number

suupaa スーパー super (fuel)

suupaa スーパー supermarket

suutsu スーツ suit

suutsu keesu スーツケース suitcase

suwarimasu 座ります v sit

suzushii 涼しい cool (temperature)

T

taaminaru ターミナル terminal (airport)

tabako 煙草 cigarette

tabako o suimasu 煙草を吸います v smoke

tabakoya 煙草屋 tobacconist

tabeamasu 食べます v eat

tabemono 食物 food

tachiiri kinshi 立入禁止 no access

tada ただ only

taika tobira 耐火扉 fire door

taipu shimasu タイプします v type

taishoku shita 退職した retired

taiya タイヤ tire/tyre [BE]

taiyoo 太陽 sun

takai 高い expensive; high

taki 滝 waterfall

takibi kinshi 焚火禁止 no fires

takushii タクシー taxi

tanima 谷間 valley

tanjoobi 誕生日 birthday

tanoshii 楽しい happy

tanoshimi 楽しみ pleasure

tanoshimimasu 楽しみます *v* enjoy

tanpon タンポン tampon

taoru タオル towel

tasuke 助け help

tasukete 助けて help me!

tatemono 建物 building

te 手 hand

teeburu テーブル table

omochikaeri お持ち帰り take-out/take away [BE]

tegami 手紙 letter/post [BE]

tekubi 手首 wrist

tenchoo 店長 manager (shop)

tenimotsu 手荷物 carry-on/hand luggage [BE]

tenimotsu hikiwatashijo 手荷物引渡所 baggage claim

tenisu テニス tennis

tenki 天気 weather

tennai no annai 店内の案内 store directory

tento テント tent

tento no shichuu テントの支柱 tent pole

tento yoo pegu テント用ペグ tent peg

terakotta テラコッタ terracotta

terebi テレビ TV

terehon kaado テレホンカード phone card

tii shatsu Tシャツ T-shirt

tisshu peepaa ティッシュペーパー tissue

tobikomimasu 飛び込みます *v* dive

todokimasu 届きます *v* reach

toire トイレ bathroom (toilet)

toire no kyuuingu トイレの吸引具 plunger

toiretto peepaa トイレットペーパー toilet paper

tokoya 床屋 barber

tokubetsuna 特別な extra

tokudai 特大 extra large

tomarimasu 止まります *v* stop

tomarimasu 泊まります *v* stay (overnight)

too 塔 tower

toochaku 到着 arrivals (airport)

tooi 遠い far

toojoo ken 搭乗券 boarding pass

toojoo shimasu 搭乗します *v* board (plane)

tooki 陶器 pottery

toonan 盗難 theft

toonyoobyoo 糖尿病 diabetic

tooza yokin 当座預金 checking account/current account [BE]

tooza yoking kooza 当座預金口座 checking account

toraberaazu chekku トラベラーズチェック traveler's check/traveller's cheque [BE]

toreenaa トレーナー sweatshirt

toreeningu jimu トレーニングジム gym

tori 鳥 bird

torikaemasu 取り替えます v exchange (goods)

torimu トリム trim (hair cut)

toshi 年 year

toshiyori 年寄り old (person)

toshokan 図書館 library

tsuaa ツアー tour

tsugi 次 next

tsukaemasen 使えません doesn't work

tsukaimasu 使います v use

tsukaisute 使い捨て disposable

tsukaisute kamisori 使い捨てカミソリ disposable razor

tsukare mashita 疲れました tired

tsukareta 疲れた exhausted

tsukemasu つけます turn on (lights)

tsukeawase 付け合わせ side dish

tsukimasu 着きます v arrive

tsuki 月 month

tsuki 付き with… (attached)

tsumaranai つまらない boring

tsume 爪 fingernail

tsumemasu 詰めます v pack

tsumemono 詰物 filling (tooth)

tsumetai 冷たい cold (food)

tsuretekimasu 連れてきます v bring

tsutsumimasu 包みます v wrap (a package)

tsuuka 通貨 currency

tsuuro 通路 aisle

tsuurogawa no zaseki 通路側の座席 aisle seat

tsuuyakusha 通訳者 interpreter

tsuzuri o iimasu つづりを言います v spell

U

ude dokee 腕時計 watch

ude 腕 arm

ueetaa ウェーター waiter

ueetoresu ウェートレス waitress

ueno 上の upper

uketorimasu 受け取ります v pick up (something)

uketsuke 受付 reception

umi 海 sea

unten menkyoshoo 運転免許証 driver's license

unten menkyoshoo bangoo 運転免許証番号 driver's license number

unten shimasu 運転します v drive

urimasu 売ります v sell

urin 雨林 rainforest

ushiro 後ろ behind (direction)

utsukushii 美しい beautiful

uuru ウール wool

W

waiaresu intaanetto ワイアレスインターネット wireless internet

waiaresu intaanetto saabisu ワイアレスインターネットサービス wireless internet service

wain risuto ワインリスト wine list

wakai 若い young

wakarimasen 分かりません I don't understand

wakarimasu 分かります v understand

wanpiisu ワンピース dress (piece of clothing)

waribiki 割引 discount

watakushi 私 I (formal)

Y

yakemasu 焼けます v burn

yakisugi 焼き過ぎ overdone

yakkyoku 薬局 pharmacy/chemist [BE]

yakyuu 野球 baseball

yama 山 mountain

yasashii やさしい easy

yasui 安い inexpensive

yatoimasu 雇います v rent/hire [BE]

yoboo sesshu 予防接種 vaccination

yodooshi 夜通し overnight

yohoo 予報 forecast

yoku yasumi mashita よく休みました well-rested

yoofukuya 洋服屋 clothing store

yooi ga dekite iru 用意ができている ready

yooshi 用紙 form (fill-in)

yoru 夜 night

yotee 予定 n schedule

yotee ni iremasu 予定に入れます v schedule

yoyaku madoguchi 予約窓口 reservation desk

yoyaku shimasu 予約します v reserve

yoyaku 予約 appointment; reservation

yubi 指 finger

yubiwa 指輪 ring

yuki no ooi 雪の多い snowy

yukigutsu 雪靴 snowshoe

yukkuri ゆっくり slowly

yurushimasu 許します v excuse

yuubin posuto 郵便ポスト mailbox/postbox [BE]

yuubinkyoku 郵便局 post office

yuuenchi 遊園地 amusement park

yuugata 夕方 evening

yuujin 友人 friend

yuukoo 有効 valid

yuusenken 優先権 right of way

yuusoo shimasu 郵送します
v mail
yuusu hosuteru ユースホステ
ル youth hostel
yuuzaa mee ユーザー名
username

Z

zasshi 雑誌 magazine
zeekan 税関 customs
zeekan shinkokusho 税関申
告書 customs declaration
form

zensai 前菜 appetizer/starter
[BE]
zensoku no 喘息の asthmatic
zero ゼロ zero
zubon ズボン pants/trousers
[BE]
zutsuu 頭痛 headache
zutsuuyaku 頭痛薬 aspirin